◇ PLAYDANCING ◇

P·L·A·Y·D·A·N·C·I·N·G

Discovering and Developing Creativity
in Young Children

Diane Lynch Fraser, Ed. D.

Assistant Professor, St. John's University
Assistant Director, School for Language
and Communication Development

A Dance Horizons Book
Princeton Book Company, Publishers

*In loving memory of my dear friend and mentor
Liljan Espenak, ADTR.
December 17, 1988.*

"To one who stepped often in the circle of life."

A Dance Horizons Book
Princeton Book Company, Publishers
POB 57
Pennington, NJ 08534

Book design by Anne O'Donnell
Cover design by Main Street Design
Typesetting by Peirce Graphic Services, Inc.
PGS/BC

Library of Congress Cataloging-in-Publication Data

Lynch Fraser, Diane.
   Playdancing : discovering and developing creativity in young
children / Diane Lynch Fraser.
     p. cm.
   Includes bibliographical references and index.
   ISBN 0-87127-153-2; ISBN 0-87127-152-4 (pbk.)
   1. Movement education—Study and teaching (Preschool) 2. Movement
education—Study and teaching (Elementary) 3. Dancing for children—
Study and teaching (Preschool) 4. Dancing for children—Study and
teaching (Elementary) 5. Creative ability in children. I. Title.
   II. Title: Playdancing.
GV452.L97   1990   90-53357
372.86—dc20

◇ *CONTENTS* ◇

Acknowledgments   vi

Introduction   viii

Foreword by Liljan Espenak   x

1 The Dancing Child: The Magical Link Between Movement and Creativity   1

2 The Playdancing Program and How It Works   7

3 The Growing Child: Looking at Development   11

4 The Creative Process   21

5 Discovering the Body   34

6 Self-Awareness: Who Am I?   44

7 Language: How Do I Tell You How I Feel?   65

8 Interpersonal Skills: Getting to Know You   89

9 The Talented Child: Identifying Giftedness   110

Afterword   114

Selected Bibliography   115

Index   119

◊ *ACKNOWLEDGMENTS* ◊

Acknowledgments are difficult. One is always afraid of ignoring someone significant. Acknowledgments are joyful. One is reminded that it is as much a privilege to thank as to be thanked. Acknowledgments are long-lasting. Those thanked will be in print for always.

To Randy, Skye, Jared, Mom and Dad, my family

To Dr. Ellenmorris Tiegerman, my friend

To Dr. Zarif Bacilious, Dr. William Sanders, Dr. Christine Radziewicz, Gladys Millman, Madeline Mando, my colleagues
                    —for their support, example, and encouragement.

To Richard Carlin, Roxanne Barrett, Debi Elfenbein, my editors
                                        —for their patience and insight.

To Lucy Anderson, Florence Lieber, Karen Crowley, Ann Mulrain, Arlene Zekowski, Jackie Ilardi, the office staff

To Janet Tammero, my secretary
                    —for their heroic efforts in typing the manuscript.

To Joan Alvarez, Colleen Murphy, Eileen Infurna, my graduate assistants
                                        —for their research.

To Margaret Tucker and the staff at Bodystrength
                                        —for their inspiration.

To the staff at the School for Language and Communication
Development, particularly Espe Arguello and Nancy Sheehan
—they live the meaning of movement each day.

To the children and parents of SLCD
—I gain knowledge every moment in their presence.

Thank you all very, very much.

D.L.F.

To Sarah Becker; Kate Brassel; Sarah Chardavoyne; Samantha Dearing;
Lizbeth Dooley-Zawacki; Timothy Ellison; Timothy Fleck; Lawrence
Goldwin; Maryann Horan; Alexis Johnson; Fiona Lopez; Juli Mulcahy;
Jackie Penney; Scott Seaman; Daniel Seminara; Nancy Sheehan; Philip
Stein; Dr. Ellenmorris Tiegman; and Matthew West who appear in the
photos in *Playdancing* and to those who appear anonymously:
Thank you.

◇ *INTRODUCTION* ◇

It is hard to believe it has been eight years since I wrote *Danceplay: Creative Movement for Very Young Children*. Since then the swaggering, smiling toddler on the cover has grown into a tall, strong, and I might add, highly creative young lady. Since then I too have grown from a young parent consulting to other young parents to a university professor and assistant director of a large private school, consulting not only to parents but to teachers, daycare facilities, community organizations, and even policy makers in government. *Danceplay* has graced the cover of *Parents* magazine and library shelves internationally. It seemed rather remote those short eight years ago that my small, seemingly simple book was bound to make such a big statement about the development of young children.

Perhaps the most profound event leading to *Playdancing* was the death of my dear friend and mentor Liljan Espenak, in 1988. She was 84 years young. It is doubtful that either *Danceplay* or *Playdancing* could have been written without her. Before she died, Liljan wrote the foreword included here. In it, she outlines her very strong belief in dance movement as a primary means of communication. Liljan was extremely distressed about the pervasive use of behavioral techniques in classrooms contrasted by the limited use of expression through the arts. Her pioneering work and writings in dance therapy allowed educators and clinicians alike to finally see the indeterminable value of movement expression, particularly for those whose communication lay "below the level of talk," like young children. The week she died she took her regular dance class at Luigi's in New York City. Liljan died as she had lived, experiencing the joys of movement.

Playdancing continues the work that Liljan began so many years ago. As she was, I am also saddened by the current absence of art and expression in preschools and the early grades in the typical early childhood setting. Children in daycare are often spending up to ten hours a day in educational environments that are potentially stimulating to creative minds and souls. Understanding and sympathetic though I am to the many problems teachers encounter, I nonetheless feel that too often energy and opportunity is wasted complaining about the lack of necessary materials and facilities. Certainly there are ways to allow children to discover and enjoy the material and environments they do have. Although I have not left parents out of *Playdancing*, my focus is on teachers. Like parents, they want to do the best job they can. But they need information, guidance, and support—just like the youngsters they are nurturing.

And so I developed *Playdancing* for the early childhood teacher. She need not leave her classroom or invest in fancy equipment to make *Playdancing* work for every child, each day. My basic philosophy about childhood education, first exposed in *Danceplay*, has not changed in these eight years. I believe the movement or "dancing" of young children has great meaning and value in their lives. It cannot and should not be ignored or trivialized. There is a natural link between the young child's spontaneous movement expression and her ability to communicate and problem solve creatively.

The activities and ideas in *Playdancing* reinforce this magical connection between movement and creativity. *Playdancing* is the result of over fifteen years of work with young children of all developmental abilities and backgrounds. It was made primarily for teachers in the classroom, but also for creative arts teachers, and parents at home. It is a carefully designed program that requires little or no dance experience—just a love of movement, ideas, and young children. ENJOY!

◇ *FOREWORD* ◇

Postural muscles are the hiding place for the emotions. Inhibition of movement limits kinesthetic awareness and perception which are essential to psychological awareness

—CHARLES DARWIN, EXPRESSIONS OF EMOTION IN MAN AND ANIMALS

Although we may receive tension from the environment, we do not store it "out there," we store it in our bodies. Without the opportunity to release this tension we become locked in certain postures and their corresponding attitudes. Our emotional repertoire becomes confined and hence, our aspiration to create ceases. We cease to feel the complete span of our emotions. What we want to achieve in our lifetime, however, is a harmony of mind and body so that the intellectual, the emotional, and the physical will work together towards a healthy, balanced individual.

Contemporary educators and psychologists have erroneously assumed movement to be separate from higher functions. They have thought of exercise as something to keep "fit" or "healthy" and grossly underestimated the role of the body as a direct link to the brain.

It is only through expressive movement (call it "dance" in its essence) that higher life expresses itself completely because it employs both mind and body. It is precisely here that we venture onto the rich territory of nonverbal communication. We do not experience another human being purely on a verbal basis. Our concept of a person is a sum total of sensation, ninety percent of which is physically communicated.

As far as intellectual functioning is concerned, we have generally associated schooling with sitting motionless at a desk for long stretches of time. But mental functioning is connected with bodily expression and dependent upon it. If this necessary cycle is broken, a child's senses will suffer and he will remain on a lower level of mental and sensory functioning.

Once society realizes that the education of small children is rooted in redirecting their physically creative capacities, the whole concept of movement will take on a new precedence. We must address the entire person, not just his mind. It is only then we can achieve the pure harmony of the human psyche that all cultures have heralded since time's beginning.

Liljan Espenak, M.A., D.T.R.
Director of Creative Therapies
New York Medical College

NOTE

Until someone invents a satisfactory genderless singular pronoun, unsatisfactory substitutes must suffice. The author has chosen to use the traditional "she" and "her," but emphasizes that this in no way reflects anything but usage, which she has been unable to improve upon, while recognizing the need for improvement.

CHAPTER 1

The Dancing Child: The Magical Link Between Movement and Creativity

Dance is older than education, and more universal, as any child instinctively knows

—LILJAN ESPENAK, DANCE THERAPY

"I'm a Tiger—a tiger, a T-T-T Tiger R-R-R-R-R- !" crooned four-and-a-half-year-old Marilise as she whirled across the carpet. Her clenched fists gradually softened and she let her arms fall gently at her sides. "But not a mean, mean tiger. No, a smiling tiger, a smiling one !" She threw her hips and elbows sideways, "R-R-R-R-R-rr," she continued.

"And I'm a pumpkin tiger, an orange pumpkin tiger," joined Marc. "A big round orange pumpkin tiger!"

"An orange pumpkin tiger, oh my!" chimed their teacher, Marie. "What does an orange pumpkin tiger do?"

"He rolls!" said Marc.

"Like a pumpkin!" said Marilise.

The two children fell to the floor rolling and singing, "I'm a tiger, a tiger, a T-T-T Tiger."

"Where does he roll?" asked Marie.

"To the M-M-M market—the market!" responded Marilise.

And so the Rolling Pumpkin Tiger dance continued for about twelve minutes. Several children joined and left as the dancers went marketing, skating, and finally for a long and well-deserved rest on the carpet.

A rolling pumpkin tiger, Marie later reflected. Not something I would have thought of.

For the young child, movement is the first and foremost vehicle through which she is able to communicate her feelings about herself and her world to others. What strikes an adult when seeing creative expression in children is their free use of the body, like the hip swaying and rolling of "pumpkin-tiger." Teachers and parents should keep in mind that for young children, dance has nothing to do with performance. It simply provides a physical aide to verbal expression. Movement is a primary mode of communication for humans and it is important that it be developed as such. The goal of *Playdancing* and all movement expression in early childhood is creative communication of feelings and ideas. Children will dance spontaneously all by themselves. But if we want them to use this movement to think more creatively and to feel better about themselves, then we need to know what to say to them, what to do, and when not to say or do anything! You see, for young children, most spontaneous movement occurs at moments of heightened emotion. Feelings and ideas come too fast for them to really understand what they are trying to say. This is why adult interpreters of the dancing child are so important.

The use of dance or movement to enhance communication or creative expression is not new. In early childhood education, in particular, it has existed by virtue of dedicated individuals under a number of aliases: eurhythmics, rhythms, singing games, and folk dance. Emerging in the early childhood curriculum as an offshoot of playground movement, the earliest dance activities in the classroom were often happenstance, occurring spontaneously with little or no interpretation or exploration by adults. If the dancing child was motivated to continue her dance, she did; in some cases another child would join her. If not encouraged, the dance would often dissolve. But whether or not anyone noticed or understood the dance, a child moving expressively is trying to communicate something about herself, about the way she sees the world. The reason she often selects movement above words for this spontaneous communication is that body movement has always been a natural outlet for expression of feeling. Creative movement is a function of our innate biological rhythms and is thus closer to natural human expression than any other art form.

The swift and joyous skip of children in play, the dragging steps of a person in grief, the forceful gait of the angry or driven, these are all the everyday observations of feelings expressed in movement. In the last analysis, every movement of the body depends upon some change in a person's feelings or purpose. Just think how unnatural it would be to think or feel and not be able to move. Even the stillness of body involved in sadness, pain, or absorption in thought involve some change in bodily posture. Therefore, anyone who proposes to work with the young dancing child needs to be aware that the medium of this work is physical and the child's direct involvement with movement is the source of her motivation to learn and communicate. In short, early education serves best when children are not alienated from physical movement tasks but are enticed to learn from them. No one needs to motivate children to climb onto a set of monkey bars. The activity in and of itself has built-in, long-term reinforcement.

Such are the benefits of Playdancing. All normally developing children can be found in their earliest years rocking back and forth to the beat of a radio, spinning in circles, or humming and vocalizing while clapping their hands. No one has shown them how to do this or even encouraged it, but almost every child does it. Young children very simply love to move! Yet Playdancing or creative movement is more than just skipping about. If it is, as I hinted before, a real form of communication, then it needs good listeners. Children dance alone only for so long. They need someone to respond to them.

Playdancing describes a variety of approaches to children, and their responses. It is a useful book for parents and teachers by merit of being a true book. It is not written as a theoretical treatise but as a real story of real children moving and learning. The book is not intended only to provide insight into creativity. It challenges some current modes that emphasize basic education devoid of art, yet offers some very practical ideas for integrating movement and the related arts into ordinary life and the early childhood curriculum.

You may be reflecting quite logically at this point, okay, movement expression may be essential for young children's creative emotional development, but *what exactly is this thing called "creative expression," and why do I want to develop it?* Although I will elaborate on this point in chapter three, I want to state right up front that although creativity is slightly related to intelligence, most research points to the fact that it constitutes a separate factor that owes little to conventional "brain power." Study after study has confirmed that individuals with high intelligence and low creativity simply do not achieve as well as those whose IQ's are lower but whose creative potential is high. This is particularly valuable information to implement when dealing with special children or so-called "slow learners." Teaching children to creatively compensate for deficits is what remediation is all about. Even so, most time in school continues to emphasize the development of conventional "intelligence," the reproduction of existing information, rather than "creativity," the capacity to invent or innovate. If we really want the world to change we must begin to build creative communicators. The arts, particularly movement, are the most joyous, evocative, and human means of approach and response. In education, as in all relationships, the intimate human approach must be sustained in a media-dominated age if we are to retain our humanity. Let's face it, when we are all senior citizens, the young children playing on our kitchen floors and skipping in our playgrounds will be our lawmakers, our decision makers. How do we want them to take care of us? Certainly not by repeating the past, but by searching creatively for solutions.

In order to develop creativity in young children, one must go beyond the traditional "flowerdance." Flowers do not only grow. They exist in gardens where they are parts of a world related to butterflies, bees, caterpillars, and worms. So, a child dancing as a flower may die because a caterpillar eats too many of her leaves, but then the caterpillar becomes a butterfly. Such dances, based upon the knowledge and thought of children, have an honesty and an immediacy that give them real beauty. The summary of feelings becomes an event in the child's life that has significance, and is a step forward in total growth for both the individual child and the child as a group member. These expressions may not look like a "dance" to an adult, and they shouldn't. The movement forms are appropriate as the ideas reflect more clearly the children who create them. Young children are not artists in the adult sense, but they can and will find ways to convey their ideas and feelings. In the effort to convey, they discover the joy of communication. Children in groups where there is plenty of creative expression have less need to drain off feelings in undesirable ways. They are likely to have fewer difficulties in working out relationships as they dance together.

Yet creative expression and communication are not the only aspects of the creative process that movement experiences enhance. Creative problem solving is also fostered. For example, one afternoon I sat observing several young children in an early childhood classroom. It was a casual enough observation. I had done this sort of thing many, many times. Tommy, a sunny, green-eyed four-year-old, was sitting over in the corner carefully spying the colorful toys on a low shelf. One by one he removed the toys, stacked them in a pile, and started what appeared to be an attempt to fit himself onto the rather confining shelf.

After several futile attempts, he walked away. I got up and walked over to Tommy.

"Finished?" I asked.

"Too hard," he replied.

"You think so?" I asked.

He did not answer, but ran back to the shelf to try once again. Tommy and I spent ten minutes on the floor folding our legs and arms in various ways, trying to exhaust the possibilities for getting him into the small cubby space. When we finally did get him in, he beamed with delight.

When I spoke to Linda, his teacher, later in the week, she said: "You know, Tommy had been looking at that cubby for weeks. I really had no idea that that's what he wanted to do. And it's interesting, he's begun all kinds of experiments with space—trying to see what things fit inside others, what things don't. I'll really have to start looking at these children more carefully."

Tommy had inadvertently proved a theory that my work has led me to believe in wholeheartedly: Physical movement has great importance in the development of creative problem solving. Once the young child learns some simple movement strategies for problem solving in one activity, she can then translate these skills to work in other activities as well. A child given the impetus to explore herself and her environment in what seems to be a purely physical sense is then freed to further explore other creative avenues—just like four-year-old Tommy was doing.

Creative problem solving is the major and essential ingredient of effective thinking. The many pressing social, political, and technological problems that face our world will best be solved by individuals who are good thinkers. It is clear from the current educational research that much time in classrooms is spent teaching information and little is devoted to teaching children how to use this information to create new ideas. How often do we hear children, who are basically good students, belabor a simple composition with the lament: I don't know what to write about.

Creative thinking or problem solving is the ability to think of many ideas, to think of unique or original ideas, or to develop elaborate ideas. Sometimes it is asking good questions which clarify a problem. It is also being able to translate ideas into forms of communication or expressions which make it possible for other people to grasp the ideas or solutions to problems. This is why movement, as a universal form of expression, is so important. It is available to every child at every stage of development.

In an increasingly complex, ever changing, challenging, and problem-ridden world, people of all ages have a great need to be good creative thinkers. And our greatest hope for improving thinking lies with our littlest thinkers.

As one young six-year-old friend, Janine, conveyed to me: "I have so many ideas I could just burst. Can't somebody help me?"

Yes, Janine; we can.

◊ CHAPTER 2 ◊

The Playdancing Program
and How It Works

*Since childhood we've used play as a means of expression, development,
and communication. When you examine it, play is a serious thing . . .
it provides a harmony of action and spirit*

RUDOLF LABAN, THE MASTERY OF MOVEMENT

Parents and teachers should not be content to wait for creativity and
problem solving to occur spontaneously in children. If you want to
foster creativity, you must be willing to take some direct action.
Playdancing differs dramatically from traditional instruction.
Customarily, the teacher alone decides what is to be learned in a
manner that may or may not meet the needs of a given child.
Playdancing allows you to accommodate each child's own special
needs in a way that reinforces the concept of putting the child first.

The basic tenet of the Playdancing program is a very simple one: that
young children have the ability to create new exciting ideas! Adults are
often blinded to this because they have difficulty comprehending
children's ideas. Yet if we are willing to expand the avenues of idea
expression beyond speaking and writing abilities to include music,
movement, and drawing, we may be surprised at what young children
are capable of expressing. Playdancing uses movement as the primary

mode of expression because this modality appears so strikingly early in development.

I have used an eclectic approach which combines movement, music, drawing, and writing in developing Playdancing because there are so many types of children. They all need a chance to learn in a way that works for them and gives them the greatest joy and motivation to continue learning. Like a tower of building blocks, Playdancing builds skill upon skill. If one block or skill is not in place, others are likely to topple. The three building blocks necessary for creative critical thinking are: self-awareness, language, and interpersonal skills.

1. Self-Awareness. Like the first block in a tower, self-awareness is a foundation skill for both language and interpersonal skills. Self-awareness refers to the ways in which young children begin to learn about their personal feelings and how to use these feelings to fulfill wants and needs. This awareness of internal states gradually appears. For example, it may not be until age five or six that children really begin to understand that the wonderfully creative things they have been thinking in their heads can actually be accomplished. Before that, children engage in fantasy for its own sake.

2. Language. Language is next in the hierarchy of creative skills because once your child has become aware of her own ideas, she has to learn to convey them to someone else. Throughout early childhood, children are developing the kinds of language skills that will allow them to express their ideas clearly. The basis for developing creative thinking depends, to a large extent, on the young child's ability to comprehend and use language skills effectively.

3. Interpersonal Skills. It may seem unusual that I have included interpersonal skills in the tower of creative development. After all, isn't creativity a solitary process? Well, yes and no. It is true that some children and adults work well away from confusion and distraction. But it is also true that once an activity is invested with social significance, the more easily and joyfully the process is learned. The final piece in the creative process is learning how to collaborate and work creatively with others.

It is important to understand that although the creative process is gradual and dependent upon the appropriate preparation, the building block analogy does not necessarily apply in the linear sense. The young child does not develop self-awareness skills entirely, move immediately on to language, and then master interpersonal skills. The three components of the creative process often overlap and in some instances occur spontaneously. The three-year-old, while highly involved in acquiring the body concept and control skills involved in self-awareness, is also learning many communication and interpersonal skills. The eight-year-old, although engaging in collaborative writing and playacting with others, is still honing information about who she is as an individual and what makes her tick. This is why I have included age-appropriate Playdances for each skill.

Each of the following chapters is concerned with a specific area of creative development. Each chapter has an introduction, a description of each Playdance, and a list of the materials needed. Activities are demonstrated for both teachers who are working with a group and for parents who are working with a single child.

Each set of Playdances is divided into two levels. Level I is geared specifically to children three to five years of age. During this period the child begins to coordinate concepts into integrated systems of thought. She is able to tell stories and paint pictures, both of which are highly developed systems of representation. It is also at this time that the young child begins to deal with abstract as well as tangible concepts. She begins to have a preliminary notion of the passing of time, how the world works and changes, and how she can orchestrate change herself. Thus, Level I Playdances are designed to help the young child enhance her growing awareness of self and to aid in the construction of abstract ideas.

Level II Playdances are designed for children six to eight years of age. During this period, the child is keenly aware that there are events taking place in the world to which she is totally invisible. There are people, places, things she has never seen and may not ever see. She knows, at least fundamentally, the limits of her own possibilities. The four-year-old doesn't know a trip to Disney World isn't *really* possible this afternoon. The seven-year-old does. This makes the seven-year-old's daily flights into fantasy not only important for critical thinking, but for overall well-being. Thus, Level II Playdances are designed for the older child not only to construct ideas but to implement them. The seven-year-old can and should be encouraged to write poetry, take photographs, and make sculpture.

Remember, Playdancing was designed to make children want to create. It also offers you a chance to share in the creative process with the child. Humans are, after all, fantastic creatures. Our vast imaginations and ability to express ourselves have helped us accomplish the very feats that separate us from all other life forms. At birth, we are among the weakest and most entirely dependent of animals, yet we can grow through our creative capacities to better the environment, to ease mental and physical pain, and to create an abundance of aesthetic wealth. Only *we* have ideas.

Note: In both Levels I and II, all exercise objectives can be converted into suitable curriculum goals. Also, most Level I Playdances can be easily adapted to the needs of Level II children.

CHAPTER 3

The Growing Child:
Looking at Development

All of Nature is found in the smallest things

—LATIN PROVERB

When considering how young children attempt to communicate creatively through movement expression, one needs to look at the whole development of the child. Each aspect of development affects all the others. Physical, emotional, social, and intellectual development are all interrelated. How children develop in each of these areas will in turn affect their creative potential. There are also broad stages in children's creative ability ranging from the purely physical or manipulative stage to one of actual movement composition or representation. The abilities that children develop at each of these stages will also affect their creativity.

◊ THE MANIPULATIVE STAGE:
THREE- AND FOUR-YEAR-OLDS ◊

This is the stage when young children engage in the freest, most spontaneous, movement explorations. It is perhaps the most important stage for here is laid the very basis for meaningful expression in the child's later development. It is the process that is of utmost importance in these early physical experiences. It does not matter how well the young preschooler kicks or leaps or spins; she is not concerned with her end product—this concern will come later in development. She is, however, concerned with exploring her repertoire of physical abilities, how her body works, and what she can do with it. She builds up this movement knowledge through experimentation. Much incidental learning takes place as the young child begins to explore the possibilities and, of course, the limitations of her own physical interaction with the environment. At the same time, she unconsciously develops preferences for certain movement styles and seeks to explore these further. She can move with others but is unable to plan collaborative effort. Her movements are often reactive to rather than deliberate within the group.

Although each three- and four-year-old is a unique individual, all possess fairly typical characteristics and needs that can feed the creative experience if handled correctly. The following table outlines specific suggestions for providing the kind of classroom environment that will help creativity to flourish.

The Three- and Four-year-old

Characteristics	Needs	Classroom Suggestions
Naturally active and energetic	Opportunities to use their whole body	Provide enough space for children to move about freely and for running, jumping, and skipping
Tire easily after periods of vigorous activity	Balance between active and quiet play	See that vigorous physical activities are followed by a story, discussion, or perhaps a snack
Express a wide range of emotions, sometimes within a short period of time	Recognition of feelings and fears	Acknowledge a wide range of emotions, including anger and sadness, through stories and discussion
Impulsive and quick to respond to situations	A safe and secure atmosphere where they are able to express emotions	When a child gets angry and hits another child, the child should be shown through actions rather than merely told alternative ways of settling the dispute

Characteristics	Needs	Classroom Suggestions
Emotional state is affected by feeling of competence. Often feel powerless, unsure, and insecure. Can have many fears	Opportunities to succeed and to develop a sense of self-esteem, belonging, and being loved	When an activity appears difficult, break it down into smaller pieces. Comfort children when necessary. Take every opportunity to use each child's name and life experiences as part of your creative curriculum
Ability to accept group life, to cooperate, and to turn-take is in its early stage	Opportunities to develop positive ways of interacting. Adult role models who are compassionate, cooperative, and who are sensitive to the child's developing social needs	Provide creative experiences that initially coax, but do not force, children into group experiences. Allow children to do things for each other
Developing an understanding of their roles	Opportunities to experience a variety of roles that they see at home and in the community	Provide costumes and dress-up clothes that stimulate dramatic play
Naturally curious. Learn best through active involvement and through their senses	Opportunities for sensory experience: to see, touch, taste, smell, and hear things around them. Opportunities to make their own discoveries	Whenever possible, provide firsthand experiences for children. If you want to talk about the ocean, bring in some sand, seashells, and seaweed
Most concerned with things that affect them personally	Opportunities to explore familiar things about their world and themselves	Provide opportunities to intently explore the familiar: soap, water, and paint. Opportunities to bring in photographs of themselves and their families, and to make their own books about their own lives should be encouraged. Stories should initially reflect feelings and ideas familiar to the children
Primarily concerned with the present, "the here and now." Developing a sense of time	Opportunities to distinguish between reality and make-believe. Opportunites to recall experiences. Opportunites to plan and organize activities	At mid-morning, children can be asked what they did earlier in the day. Each day, the children should be asked where and with what they want to work

Characteristics	Needs	Classroom Suggestions
Developing the ability to symbolize experiences	Opportunities to express ideas in a variety of forms such as stories and music	All Playdances are classroom suggestions here
Developing the ability to deal with complex, abstract ideas	Opportunities to note similarities and differences between things around them. Opportunities to sort, group, categorize, and classify	Children can be asked to compare or contrast any two familiar items in terms of color, size, or functions

◊ THE SYMBOLIC STAGE: FIVE- AND SIX-YEAR-OLDS ◊

Suzanne Langer, the philosopher, once advanced a theory that human beings are born with an urgent biological need to talk, draw, paint, sculpt, make music, and—yes—dance because they need to deal with the meaning of their experience at a distance. By drawing a picture of it or making a dance about it, we are able to clarify the

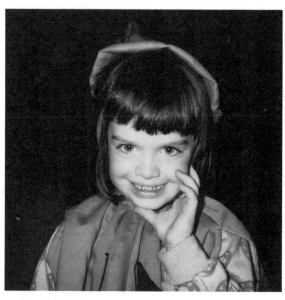

Usually, there is a complete lack of frustration on the part of the child who feels herself to be in command of the situation.

experience for ourselves. The five-year-old's dance is no longer the simple release of energy and expression it is for the three-year-old. The kindergarten dance has a much deeper meaning than the one performed in preschool.

It is thrilling to watch young children as they begin their first truly symbolic movement expressions. They will confidently set out to move like some particular thing and be quite satisfied with their efforts. Usually, there is a complete lack of frustration on the part of the child who feels herself to be in command of the situation. Indeed, a five-year-old can say, I am going to be an ogre, and may confidently dance something quite unintelligible as an ogre for another. Yet for her, she has definitely symbolized this hideous monster.

Once young children realize that they can create whatever they desire, they will often spend longer periods at a symbolic activity and do several dances revolving about the same idea. This kind of dancing is quite different from the three-year-old who really cannot be said to dance about anything. The three-year-old dances to feel the joy of physical movement; the five-year-old dances to feel the joy of ideas in movement. Children in the symbolic stage begin to move cooperatively with each other; although, planned dances or compositions will evolve later.

The Five- and Six-year-old

Characteristics	Needs	Classroom Suggestions
Learning to control their bodies	Opportunities to demonstrate muscle control	Provide movement activities that emphasize muscle and/or impulse control such as "statues," run-and-stop, or seeing how long they can stand on one foot
Developing concentration and can pay attention to a single activity for as long as 15–20 minutes	Opportunities to be engaged and absorbed by activities that require longer attention	See that children are allowed to explore materials for as long as they need. Give them time to develop their emerging concentration. Make certain the classroom is filled with interesting, attention-getting materials
Able to talk about their strengths and weaknesses. Get embarrassed or frustrated	Opportunites to know that making a mistake is okay. Opportunities to repair their own errors	Provide experiences where children can learn to correct their own errors or inconsistencies. Help

Characteristics	Needs	Classroom Suggestions
when they don't do something "right"		children explore problems by asking, How does that feel/look/sound to you? How could you fix that?
Beginning to suggest taking turns during group play	Opportunities to engage in turn-taking activities	Provide experiences where children are asked both to take turns and request turns of other children
Respond to directions that have three to four sequenced steps	Opportunities to engage in complex activities that involve specific directions	See that children engage in activities that involve the handling of simple directions, e.g., recipes, fundamental origami
Have many emotions, some of which are displayed appropriately; beginning to respond with empathy to others' feelings	Opportunities to handle emotionally charged situations with less intervention from adults	Provide children with experiences and stories that depict individuals in social/emotional predicaments
Beginning to demand more realism in play experiences	Opportunities to stimulate real-life situations	Provide children with time to playact situations they have actually experienced
Interested in receiving adult attention; may "show off"	Opportunities to receive adult attention	See that children receive attention for tasks both big and small; try not to relegate attention to the "big moments"
Developing a sense of humor	Opportunities to report and comment upon life's inconsistencies, the "funny things"	Allow children to create and tell their own jokes and humorous stories
Beginning to form their first real friendships	Opportunities to initiate and engage in play with preferred playmates	Although children should experience the company of all or most class members, accommodations should be made so children can be special friends at certain points during the day
May play independently, but still need tremendous support and comfort from adults	Opportunities to be comforted and supported when feeling inadequate	Provide children with stories that emphasize acceptance of all feelings, including fear and anxiety

◊ THE REPRESENTATIONAL STAGE: SEVEN- AND EIGHT-YEAR-OLDS ◊

For many years the early elementary school has been concerned with providing creative experiences for children. Seven- and eight-year olds are highly capable individuals who need time and space to construct their own realities rather than merely relying upon prefabricated tasks. Many children this age can read and write quite well. Some can play musical instruments and perform preliminary classical dance steps. It is at this age of seven and eight that parents are encouraged to begin a child's formal training in athletics, painting, or piano. Yet it is not this formal training in sports or the creative arts that *Playdancing* emphasizes here. There are certain children who demonstrate a natural inclination or talent for artistic expression, and these will be discussed later, in chapter nine. But all seven- and eight-year olds, specially gifted or not, need to continue the development of creative expression and problem solving begun in their preschool years.

Interestingly enough, most educational research indicates that it is in the fourth grade, the year following this second/third grade period, that the greatest drop in young children's creative activity occurs. Some theories advance the notion that it is peer pressure, the tremendous urge to conform, that is responsible for this drop. Although I cannot belittle the impact of social pressure at any age or stage, the gradual change in teaching methods and materials during the early elementary grades also play a part. Children sit a great deal more in second grade than they do in kindergarten. By the time the child enters the third grade, there is a tremendous emphasis on the right answer as opposed to an original or thoughtful one. Children do not need *less* stimulation because they are older; they need *more* complex, *more* challenging stimulation!

The dancing seven- and eight-year-old is mentally able to construct her inner world using movement. The three-year-old cannot do this; neither can the five-year-old. The eight-year-old can map out a real movement composition replete with passages into her unconscious mind. By just sitting quietly and motionless on the carpet, she can reach deeply inside herself and understand what it is like to feel the sun on her face, wear the shoes of a princess, or embrace a loved one. Movement can enhance learning and introduce children to ideas they might never encounter otherwise. Teachers can tap into these newly developing abilities in social studies, science, and literature.

The Seven- and Eight-year-old

Characteristics	Needs	Classroom Suggestions
Highly developed large and small muscle control, and in some cases, skill and coordination	Opportunities to capitalize on muscle skill in non-competitive arenas	Teachers should deviate from the traditional races and competitive games of this developmental period to support alternative roads to physical competence. All Playdances support physical exploration and muscle control without continual emphasis on strength or power
Can concentrate on selected activities for indefinite periods	Opportunities to select and complete chosen projects	All curriculum should support activities that are individually selected
Understand and experience a wide range of emotions. Know when and how to express feelings appropriately; although, they may not always reflect this knowledge	Opportunities to acknowledge true feelings appropriately	Provide experiences in role playing. For example, ask, What would you do if . . . ? or How do you think you'd feel if . . . ?
Aware of and capable of complying with many social rules and expectations	Opportunities to understand when it would be important to exercise rules and when it could be important to break them	Provide initial storylines in playacting activities that do not have simple answers, such as: The man on the street says he's hungry; should I give him my bus fare? or My sister's puppy is very sick; should the veterinarian put him to sleep?
Can represent internal experiences, and have codified fantasies. Can place themselves mentally into situations they have never actually experienced	Opportunities to represent internal events	Provide opportunities for children to represent fantasies. For example, ask, What do you think it would be like to fly, to visit another planet, to tap dance on mustard, or to turn into clay?
Interested in what other people think and what they do	Opportunities to continually explore their ability to take a perspective	Always allow children to see, hear, and experience other points of view. Give all children the same theme and see how each individual develops it. Continually nurture and

Characteristics	Needs	Classroom Suggestions
		encourage exchange of ideas
Can work very well collectively	Opportunities for teamwork and collaborative effort	Set aside time for children to work in pairs and in small groups of three. Once they have become facile here, it is easier for them to work in larger groups
Have formulated a self concept	Opportunities to redefine and explore who they are	Have children recognize and support all the things that happen to them. Have them keep a journal: standard diary form, or one of poems, photographs, and pictures, or one of relevant stories
Able to give more thought to judgments or decisions	Opportunities to reflect on activities	Have children go back to earlier projects and reconstruct them, repair them, or make them better
Learning to forego immediate reward for delayed gratification	Opportunites to plan and execute long-term projects	Have children self-select individual or group themes to be developed over the course of several weeks

Most young children are as eager to learn to read, write, and count as they are to jump and run or sing out loud. Yet the prolonged inactivity that accompanies book learning in many classrooms can create real tension. Amazingly, many children make whatever personal adjustments are necessary in their school situations. They learn to suppress their feelings of discomfort, to understand that in the classroom their wishes are not as important as they once thought, and to accept others' goals instead of searching for their own. Yet that level of adoption should not be the goal of learning.

Developmentally, nothing prepares the average seven-year-old for the often dynamic shift to motionless "activity" that accompanies transfer to school-age life. However, the advantages of joy and playfulness in learning are as important at eight as they are at three. The creativity in play that contributes to a child's positive self-image at age four contributes to her ability to communicate effectively with peers at age seven.

Preserving a child's artistic and self-expressive instincts throughout the early childhood years is not easy. There are many counter-expectations from others. Although more accepting of unique expressions at age three-and-a-half and four, parents may want children to send home fairly standard constructions of Easter bunnies and apple trees by the time they are six. A teacher must have very firm beliefs not to follow suit and engage in teaching practices that diminish the likelihood of learning experiences that promote creative development at all ages and stages. Pressure can also come from the children themselves who, in the later years, may want to do more "grown-up" things or make items "correctly."

Teachers must remember that a child's confidence in creative experience once lost is almost always difficult to retrieve. Self concepts are actually quite fragile and need time to develop resiliency. Providing continual experiences for children's creative growth requires patience and committment. Effort is rewarded, however, by the continual flow of energy and ideas.

CHAPTER 4

The Creative Process

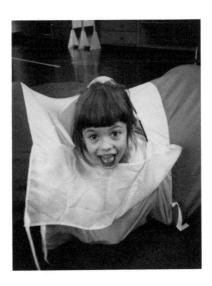

With our foolish and pedantic methods we are always preventing children from learning what they could learn much better by themselves while we neglect what we alone can teach them

JEAN-JACQUES ROUSSEAU, THE PROPHETIC VOICE

The creative being does not emerge suddenly. She develops gradually and grows by meeting problems, recognizing them, and being able to direct them successfully. Participation in children's learning activities can contribute to the emergence of this creative person. Curiosity is a primary motivating force in children. Teachers need to provide a rich variety of firsthand experiences to be explored and acted upon. The desire for love and appreciation is also a strong motivating force. It is a need that can easily be exploited unless we keep clearly in mind the child's purposes and her level of development. Too often one may be concerned with his own purposes rather than with the child's. If we give the child approval only for what is good by our standards, we may be limiting her creative development as an individual in her own right.

To foster creativity in children, teachers must be adequate, fully functioning people. According to some researchers, such people have the following characteristics:

- a positive view of self
- an identification with others
- openness to experience and acceptance
- a rich and available perceptual field

The support role of the truly creative teacher is an important one. She gives support to the child by showing an interest in what the child does, by treating the child's questions with respect, by giving more attention to the positive than to the negative aspects of the child's performance, and by giving generous, real approval for real accomplishment.

Perhaps no person has advocated the significance of the creative process in early childhood more than physician and educator Maria Montessori. In early childhood, the child acquires an overwhelming abundance of knowledge that will prepare her for the rest of her life. Before Montessori, educators believed that learning began at age six. They were correct in assuming this because the methods they employed were effective only for children who had reached the so-called "age of reasoning." They had neglected to note, however, that somehow children assimilate a wealth of material that they could never again duplicate before entering elementary school. They have learned a mass of coordination skills, a pattern of cultural and social adjustments, and all the nuances of a highly sophisticated language. The reason for this, according to Montessori, is that the young child's conscious and subconscious states have not yet separated. Young children experience the world totally and do not yet possess a governing superego restricting what they can or cannot do. Their minds are open and all absorbing. Society had overlooked the child's inherent need for creative experience. As Montessori observed:

> The crying of children is a problem in Western countries. How often do we hear parents complain of their children's incessant crying? The reply of modern psychology is this: "The baby cries and becomes disturbed, has screaming fits and rages because he is suffering from mental hunger." And this is the truth. The child is bored. He is being mentally starved, kept prisoner in a confined space offering nothing but frustrations to the exercise of his powers. The only remedy is to release him from solitude, and let him join in social life[1]

[1]Montessori, Maria. *The Absorbent Mind.* New York: Dell Publishing, 1967.

22

If a child's creative resources are taken from her, the mind will have no alternative but to become vacant. If human personality is formed during the early years of life, children deprived of this creative process can be cheated out of their own mental health. Yet when teachers or parents excite a child's fantasies through the use of music, props, or stories, they quite inadvertently stimulate this essential, creative-developmental process. Several pieces of ribbon thrown casually on the floor may become a brook one can jump over; a bright piece of music becomes the background for the child to stab her fists into the air; or a circus story may invoke a herd of elephants. The creative process can be viewed, very simply, as change in both thinking and action. Many obstacles to creative thinking are simply emotional

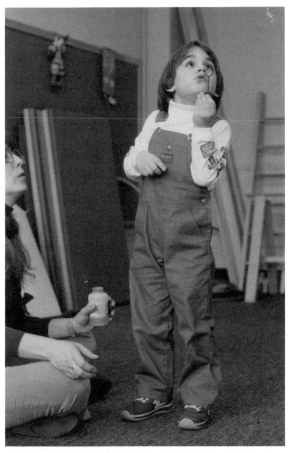

Teachers and parents have a very specific role in this creative inquiry process. They need to provide the child with the initial experience or concept worthy of investigation.

reactions to insecure feelings that are caused by fear of new or different ideas. By suggesting novel ideas people open themselves up to criticism. If is often easier to conform than to risk making a fool of oneself.

Yet the creative process is learned, just like anything else. What needs to change most dramatically is one's perception of learning. Traditionally, one is thought to know something only if she can reproduce existing information. And this information needs to be reproduced while sitting motionless at a desk. Questions must have answers, and these answers must be definitive. Yet in order to inspire creative learning, the only questions that should be asked are those without definitive answers. Teachers and parents have a very specific role in this creative inquiry process:

- they need to provide the child with the initial experience or concept worthy of investigation
- they need to provide the materials to begin the avenues of exploration
- they need to provide information sources for the child's questions
- they need to provide reinforcement

In order to help children become good thinkers, we need to give them something to think about. Questions can be the springboard for creative expression if they offer a number of viable options. For young children, pure fantasy is often the best catalyst. For example, the teacher might ask, Let's pretend there is an elephant asleep in the playground, how do you think we could get it into the classroom?

The teacher can either take a large sheet of paper or use a chalkboard to record all the options children generate ranging from rolling the elephant on a giant skateboard to using a magic wand to make it disappear outside and reappear in the classroom. Children could then be divided into small groups, each with a separate Playdance to orchestrate.

Older children can be posed the same kind of question, giving the same fantastic solutions. Yet their orientation to reality requires us to add a final step. These children can be asked to reflect on their Playdances and evaluate what Playdance is in fact the most practical, what one the most outrageous. In this way, they begin to assess their own thinking processes.

Now, you may be thinking all well and good, but when are children realistically going to be confronted with such outlandish problems?

The answer: just about every day. Every time they stare at you, paper in hand, with nothing to say, or after school with nothing to do. Children need adult models to begin the rehearsal of the creative thinking process for themselves.

◇ PRACTICAL CURRICULUM SUGGESTIONS ◇

Original efforts involving the specific teaching of critical thinking and problem-solving at a definite time and place in the classroom prove futile. Much time in early childhood classrooms is devoted to the teaching of basic skills: language arts, reading, math, and science. Thus, Playdancing is incorporated into the general curriculum and gives teachers information on how to encourage the creative process within their regular curriculum as much as possible.

Parents at home will also find that it is more beneficial to use Playdancing as a part of their ordinary routine, rather than setting up some artificial premise for these activities. Both teachers and parents need to be sensitized to a child's cues for when given Playdances are ready to begin and, likewise, ready to end. Ten minutes for one child in one Playdance might be plenty. Another child may need twice that long. When children lose attention or become fatigued, it is always time to stop. If teachers or parents are uncertain, *ask the child.* Children can be surprisingly articulate about their wants and needs if you give them the chance to explain their feelings.

Here are some general suggestions for creating an atmosphere conducive to the creative process both in the classroom and at home:

1. *Support and reinforce unusual ideas and responses.* Once during circle time, a kindergarten teacher asked, "So what did everyone have for dinner last night?" One little boy, Robbie, volunteered, "Oh, we went to the place where they put whales in our drinks." Now the teacher could have removed herself from this completely. She had wanted to talk about healthy foods verses foods that were not so healthy—but she didn't. It turned out that this particular child had been to a rather unusual restaurant with his parents where they actually did have various forms of plastic marine life floating in their drinks. Kathy, the teacher, soon had everyone in the class floating about. They floated, swam, wriggled. This initial creative

experience spawned a number of subsequent ones in which children were motivated to bring in books on marine life from home, and collected a wide array of seashells which they used as inspiration for a whole host of Playdances.

Kathy herself began to explore and discovered a number of interesting facts about the seaworld that she would probably never have discovered on her own. Did you know that male seahorses reproduce; that sharks never stop moving; that a horseshoe crab is really not a crab at all, but a form of spider? Many teachers, unlike Kathy, would have silenced Robbie's comment about the whales and moved directly onto those aspects which related to her "healthy food" curriculum. And, oh, what would have been missed! Teachers and parents really need to listen to children. Children are not empty slates that must be filled with ideas we consider important. They are wonderfully full vessels of fresh ideas.

2. *Use failure as a positive to help children realize new strategies.* A first grade class was building models of tepees as part of their social studies curriculum. Carrie, a little girl, simply could not get her tepee to stand. It kept toppling over, much to her distress and dismay.

Evelyn, her teacher, came over:

"It's not working, is it, Carrie?"

"It's stupid," answered Carrie.

"Well, how could you fix it?"

"I don't know."

Evelyn had the class come together. She stood away from the class with her legs two feet apart and her arms parallel to the floor. "Okay, now someone try to push me down!" shouted Evelyn.

Try as they could, Evelyn stood solid. Giggling and laughing, the children begged to each have a turn to be pushed. After about fifteen minutes of this, the children returned to work and Carrie and Evelyn returned to the tepee. Carrie's tepee was tall and thin with little base to support it—no wonder it toppled! Carrie carefully took her tepee apart and started experimenting with new ways to keep it supported.

Now Evelyn could have just as easily given Carrie this information: make the base wider. But Carrie wouldn't have understood why and more than likely would not have been as motivated to experiment with new strategies. By giving Carrie information the physical way, Carrie and all the other children in the classroom had truly integrated some of the fundamental aspects of balance.

3. *Allow children to have choices and be part of the decision-making. Let them have a part in the control of their learning experiences.* Barbara had thought another reading of *Where the Wild Things Are* would excite her four-year-olds. This age group loves both repetition and monsters. However, upon presenting the reading, Barbara found that this group was really interested in talking about their own monsters. Group decision warranted Barbara putting her book away and giving way to a different kind of language activity.

One by one each child was given the opportunity to talk about and move just like her monster. Additional activities involved the construction of monster costumes and a final theatrical production of monster Playdances. Barbara later reflected on this experience: " I have to admit that most of the meat for the production came from the kids. And because the activities were theirs, and not mine, their motivation was extremely high. Some children were able to work for incredibly long periods of time—an hour or more!"

Most research has shown that when child activities are self-selected, attention spans are high, even for four-year-olds. The trick is to motivate a group in the right direction—not tell them what to do, but stir their curiosity.

◇ GETTING THE CREATIVE PROCESS STARTED ◇

One important way of establishing a classroom atmosphere for creative learning is through careful attention to the physical arrangements of the classroom. You will probably discover that it is useful to designate various parts of the classroom for a number of individual or group activities during the day. If your room is large enough, you may want to use dividers to partition your room into various activity areas: a large carpeted area for group Playdances and discussion, smaller spaces for clusters of children to work, and a special area for quiet relaxation and thinking. Creative ideas often require a period of time for incubation.

You must keep in mind that Playdancing obviously requires a greater degree of physical activity and discussion than that required by more traditional activities, particularly of the seat-work variety. In

A stimulating classroom is filled with resources. There are things to explore, read, study, and examine.

your effort to develop a supportive environment for creative learning, do not work against your own purposes by being too rigid about movement, activity, and noise. There is an important difference, which you can soon learn to distinguish, between disruptive behavior and the productive noise and activity of children busily involved in tracking down new ideas and solutions to problems.

A stimulating classroom is filled with resources. There are things to explore, read, study, and examine. There are places to relax and talk. The teacher encourages children to talk, to move about, to share ideas. Children do not drift aimlessly. There is no chaos. There is, however, much active pursuit of learning activities. But the atmosphere should nonetheless remain relaxed and pleasant. It is only in such a classroom that the creative process can flourish.

When you first begin the Playdancing program, select a content area you are already comfortable with, such as language arts, science, or music. Then take a look at the activities in Chapters five through eight, and pick out something you like. You do not have to swallow the entire Playdancing program in whole; just take a little piece at a time. Watch for a time during your regular classroom planning when this activity could possibly be put in, then go ahead, and try it! Remember to be patient with yourself and your class. Change takes time.

When teachers first begin to consider the efforts of increased student participation in planning, and greater student independence in learning, it is easy for some misunderstanding to occur. Quite frequently, for example, an atmosphere for the creative process is confused with a totally unstructured or permissive environment. The proper implementation of Playdancing is more likely to lead to children working concentratedly toward important goals and objectives, and less likely to lead to incidences of aggressive or disruptive behavior.

The teacher always maintains a low authority profile and acts as a guide or facilitator of activities. Relaxing control may be difficult for some teachers, but it is usually an essential ingredient in getting children to think for themselves. At first, students may not be productive. Remember, children need time to adjust just as much as adults do. Do not give up if your first attempts are rough around the edges. Give yourself a fair chance to develop your own creative abilities. Too many times educational projects are dismissed prematurely, with the first signs of difficulty, only later to have someone say, Oh, I tried that once but it didn't work out. You must not be overcome with the frustration of a first attempt, but remember that with more experience, success can be attained.

Playdancing, like any other educational concern, can be handled in such a way as to become a dull, boring routine. Your children will need variety and there will be a constant pressure on you, as well as upon them, to create new ideas. Playdancing is not a venture for the teacher who wants to build a neat little package to use day in, day out. You will have to work very hard to be flexible and original yourself. You will also have to learn to be flexible in your response to children. You will not have the cushion of the right answers in the teacher's guide to fall back upon. There are times you will simply have to say, I don't know, and these situations can be threatening to some people.

You must be prepared to create and maintain a growing pool of resources for learning. It will not do to simply put the goblins and witches up on the bulletin board in October and leave them until the turkeys go up in November. There will be many different resources, and you will have to work hard to see that they are up-to-date and well suited to the ever evolving interests of your children. When children bring materials from home, do not opt for the old standby of, leave it in your cubby. You need to be prepared to bring each child's interests right into the classroom. But remember, you need to set the pace at first. Once your children see you bringing in and using interesting and unusual materials, they will do the same. At first, it may be difficult to keep in mind that all children have the potential for creative thinking. One cannot be concerned with the few children who display exceptional creative talent, but with providing opportunities for all children to develop their abilities and interests.

◇ THE THREE PHASES OF THE CREATIVE PROCESS ◇

Idea Awareness: Sensing that an idea exists
Idea Formation: Defining and exploring the idea
Idea Reflection: Evaluating the idea

The creative process cannot be viewed as a single event, it is a process of overlapping steps. First, one recognizes an idea or problem; secondly, one thinks of the possible avenues for exploration; and lastly, one evaluates these avenues. This process of inquiry most normally begins when children question something about their experience. The teacher can and should structure children's learning so that they do question. Once they question, which, in fact, is the act of recognizing an idea, then the entire creative process is set in motion. Intrinsic interest takes hold, and learning by discovery takes place. Every *Playdancing* exercise in each creative development area, whether it be self-awareness, language, or interpersonal skills, operates on this principle. Every exercise involves a questioning, exploring, and evaluation or discussion phase.

Idea Awareness

It is perhaps during this initial phrase that teachers and parents can have the most input into the Playdancing process. Remember, in order for children to think creatively, they need something to think about. Children may not even be aware that they have an idea unless someone helps them organize their thinking. Sometimes something as simple as an interesting picture or book can be a catalyst.

For example, Kim was watching a group of three-year-olds standing at the water table. She had placed a number of objects around the warm water: spoons, plastic trays, cups, and several bars of soap. Children were happily pouring soapy water back and forth, from one cup to another, dripping warm water down the front of their taut, plastic aprons. Lynne, one of the group, began to notice how sticky the soap was becoming. She began to squeeze it between her hands until it flattened and separated into several long strips between her fingers. She then began to pick up the strips of soap she had created, each time squeezing it in a like fashion.

Kim went over to Lynne and asked, "Oh my, what's happening to the soap?"

"It's icky."

"Yes, it is."

"Was the soap icky when I took it out of the package?"

"No."

" I wonder why."

Kim began to remove the sticky strips of soap from the water and press them into tiny balls. Lynne followed her, as did several other children.

Lynne suggested, "Let's see what happens when we put the soap into the freezer."

Kim led her tiny group down the hall and into the kitchen where they all placed their soap into the freezer. "Let's wait a while and see what happens," said Kim.

The children all marched back to their classroom and resumed other activities. About an hour later Kim took her group back to the kitchen, removed the tiny balls of soap from the freezer, placed them on a large wooden cutting board, and took them back to the classroom. Back in the classroom, Kim placed the cutting board with the soap down on a table. She picked a soap ball up and threw it down on the board. It shattered into many tiny splinters. Soon every child in the room was around the table begging for a turn.

This activity soon evolved into a series of Playdances involving the concept of soft and hard, and the scientific concept of mass in general. Children stiffened their bodies into tight little packages, only to relax and fall into soft little piles on the floor. Three-year-olds need concrete experience to realize relationships. Notice Kim placed herself in the role of explorer, as well as asking her children to do so. She could not say to the children, the reason the soap is getting soft is because water or any liquid has less mass than soap. Mass is not a concept available to most children at the abstract level. She had to allow the class to discover this relationship between object and environment for themselves.

Idea Formation

Once children realize that there is an idea to explore, the essential movement activity of Playdancing can begin. Again, the teacher or parent needs to be very astute here and direct the line of questioning so that the children themselves can begin to clarify ideas. For example, Paul, a bright four-year-old, was sitting on the carpet with a wide assortment of interlocking Lego pieces. Instead of stacking them one upon another as they were designed to be used, Paul was lining them up in domino fashion, making long swirling designs on the floor. After several minutes of this, Paul sat back from his floor designs and began to examine them. He went over to his teacher, Beth, and said, "Look, Beth; look at all the letters!"

Beth came over with several other children and soon everyone was standing looking at Paul's swirling designs. "Paul says he sees letters here, let's help him find them. When you find a letter, stop, and let us all see."

As each child found a letter, Beth had her lie down next to or near the shape and form the shape with her body. As each child made a shape, Beth encouraged further exploration by having alternate children form the same letter shapes in different ways. After children had seemingly exhausted possibilities, Beth took further initiative by dividing the Lego pieces and placing them in several containers about the classroom. Later in the day, several children began to experiment on their own, laying the Lego pieces out on the carpet and trying to form their own Lego shapes. In some cases, a twosome would form, and children would try to imitate a design together. An infinite number of Playdances evolved from this initial activity, with children using a variety of design material like a tape, yarn, and pipe cleaners to make a like variety of exciting shapes.

Idea Reflection

The final phase of the Playdancing process involves reflecting upon what has happened. This usually involves some type of discussion. In some cases, certain forms of exploration may have proved more fruitful than others. The question here obviously is why. One of the more advanced intellectual abilities of human beings is their ability to reflect upon and reconstruct the past. No other animal can do this. Even high order primates, like chimpanzees, rely heavily on instinct for their behavior. This last step in the Playdancing process is crucial for the integration of ideas.

When Peggie's second grade class had finished their Playdances on human emotion, she brought all the children together on the carpet. "Okay, what do you know now that you didn't know before?" Peggie sat with a large yellow legal pad and transcribed anything and everything the children said:

"Well, I thought being scared was the same as being anxious."

"You know, being angry is kind of like being excited."

"Feeling tired can make you feel sad."

These comments triggered new associations and, in some cases, more fuel for future Playdances. Teachers need to leave adequate time for this final step. The way this last step is handled can insure how the knowledge from the Playdancing process is translated into children's everyday lives.

Using the Playdancing program involves some important decisions about your own values and commitments. Teachers need to make primary the fostering of personal creative growth for each child. Teachers cannot view their job as mechanical or as merely the imparting of specific pieces of knowledge. The commitment to help children think better is a serious one, yet Playdancing can make it extremely stimulating and fulfilling.

◇ CHAPTER 5 ◇

Discovering the Body

I experience my body as uniquely and peculiarly my own. My body is intimately related to what and who I am

CALVIN O. SHRAG, ART AS THERAPY

"Okay, everyone, let's sit down on the floor and close our eyes. Hands on knees and sitting straight—like an arrow. Listen; listen to your breathing in and out, in and out. That's it; that's it. Quiet; quiet . . . Move your tummy in and out. Slowly; slowly."

[After five minutes]

"Sissy, are you beating a drum?"

"Silly, Jeremy, that's your heart!"

Even the youngest child has an enormous love and respect for the wonderful body she inhabits. To be in tune and in touch with one's body helps free a child from doubt about herself and gives her confidence. For the young child, simple actions like rolling over and over again, or getting up very, very slowly, or pretending to be extremely heavy help her gain coordination control while simultaneously discovering the wonder that is her body.

Each body and its movements are individual. It is doubtful whether any movement by one body could be duplicated exactly by another. The individuality of each body and its movements provides one of the ways in which young children begin to see themselves as distinct personalties. It is one of the ways in which they communicate their individuality to others.

Although philosophers like Calvin Shrag recognize the importance of body awareness to intellectual development, the body is simple and primary for the very young child. Even so, many children, perhaps due to culture or personality, learn to divorce themselves from fundamental bodily experiences. They do not know when they are tense or relaxed. They cannot find a comfortable position when seated on the floor. They maneuver awkwardly in spaces, continually bumping into, stepping on, or spilling things. Although a general clumsiness can be viewed as part of the normal growing process, these body-divorced children act as if their bodies were not really part of them at all!

Without a real investment in basic body exploration, movement expression and communication can be very frustrating, if not downright difficult, for children. Very frequently, children describe what they have seen, heard, or felt by means of reenacting the situation. Long before school age, the small child will recall the pleasures of the summer by repeating them over and over again through bodily movement. Victor, age five, was having difficulty with this and sat for hours in the book corner trying to find pictures that could describe his summer vacation:

> *Victor:* It's not here! It's not here! Ah! I am so mad! [collapsing on the floor]
> *June:* No, Victor. It is here right inside you.
> *Victor:* No, no! I'm going to forget and then it is going to be gone.
> *June:* Well, Victor, since you are lying down, let's close our eyes. Now, do you know what we're going to do?
> *Victor:* What! Squeeze my eyes—like this?
> *June:* No; no. Soft closing—not tight. We're going to keep your brain awake and put your body to sleep, and then your brain is going to make pictures.
> *Victor:* Like a movie?
> *June:* No, more like a dream.

June firmly placed her hand on various parts of Victor's body to "put them to sleep." Children often respond readily to this form of mental suggestion. His brain began to make just the right pictures, like June had said. Subsequent to this, Victor was often seen sitting quietly with his eyes closed. "Picture time," he called it.

Incidents that have puzzled children or caused some fear can also be reexamined in this way. Although children renew pleasurable experiences, like Victor, more often they are trying to understand events more clearly by repeating them. Children are assailed by impressions, accepted as humdrum by adults, that are fresh, even overwhelming, to them. All this welter of experience, if it is to mean anything to them, must be externalized, sorted, and then stored or discarded in some way. Playing out an experience through bodily movement is the most immediate way young children have of externalizing experiences in order to examine them. However, the child locked in her own under-sensitized body is not going to be easily availed of these experiences. Victor, for example, had to learn to relax his body before he could make pictures.

The following exercises are the foundation of the Playdance program. Without being aware of the workings of her body, it is doubtless a child can really communicate or create to her full potential. The best way to become aware of the body is to look at it and see how it works. What is particular about your individual model?

◇ FUNDAMENTAL PLAYDANCES: AGES THREE TO FIVE ◇

Exercise 1.
Breathing In and Out

> OBJECTIVE: To develop awareness of one's breathing and ability to relax.

> WHEN TO DO: Early in the Playdance program, perhaps as the first exercise introduced. Particularly applicable prior to naptime or after a vigorous activity.

> DESCRIPTION: For groups or individuals: Ask the children to lie down on their backs, close their eyes, and pretend to fall asleep. Tell them to imagine a black velvet curtain descending over their eyes, or that their bodies are floating on water—any image that relaxes them. Initially, some children may indeed fall asleep.
>
> When everyone is lying still, tell them to listen to your voice, but to keep their eyes closed. Speak in a calm, but natural, tone of voice. Tell them to begin to breathe the way they do when they are asleep. If they are quiet and relaxed you can go on to the next fundamental exercise. If they are jumpy or giggly,

they are telling you they have had enough, and you
should move on to something else.

Exercise 2.
Body Finding

OBJECTIVE: To develop awareness of individual body parts.

WHEN TO DO: Early in the Playdance program, as one of the first
exercises introduced.

DESCRIPTION: For groups: Start with the "Breathing In and Out"
exercise. When the children are lying on their backs,
relaxed but alert, tell them that they are going to
move each part of their body, one at a time,
beginning with their toes. They should keep their
eyes closed and feel their body move.

Ask them to lift one foot off the floor. Wiggle the
ankle. Put the foot down. Now lift the other foot.
Wiggle the ankle. Put the foot down. Now wiggle all
ten toes.

Lift one leg again. Bend the knee in and out, in and
out. Now lift the other leg and bend the knee in and
out, in and out. Remember to speak and move calmly
yourself while giving instruction. The tone and
rhythm of your voice is key in facilitating this
relaxation experience.

Continue, repeating your instructions for the arms
and head. Have the children twist their wrists, wiggle
their fingers, bend their elbows, and circle, nod, and
tilt their heads. If they are sufficiently relaxed, you
might ask them to circle their shoulders or feel their
stomachs go in and out. When a child appears to be
having difficulty, go to that child and place your hand
on the indicated body part. This simple gesture can
often give a child the needed touch information to
continue the exercise.

Children should not be expected to complete this
entire series of individual body movements the first
time around. Some children will need more time than
others. If children get restless, do not push. This
defeats the entire purpose of the exercise. Finish up
gradually and try again tomorrow.

For individuals: Go through the same routine as you would for a group. With a single child, you will simply have more opportunity for hands-on instruction. You might want to touch each individual body part before asking your child to move it.

Exercise 3.
Me and My Shadow

OBJECTIVE: To develop awareness of one's body and how it moves.

WHEN TO DO: Early in the Playdance program, particularly if a child quite incidentally discovers her shadow.

MATERIALS NEEDED: Large flashlights, several lamps, or small penlights.

DESCRIPTION: For groups: Dim the classroom lighting and ask children to search for shadows. Once they have discovered some, begin to cast shadows on the walls with your flashlight or lamp offering as little distortion as possible. Move the light farther from the body and your shadow is bigger, move it closer, your shadow is little. When children move, have them really inspect what they do. How can they move differently? What happens when they jump or stand on one foot, wave their arms, or spin on one foot?

If you have enough small penlights for everyone, distribute them and have each child inspect her shadow individually.

For individuals: Use the same process as you would for a group. You might want to work as a pair. Your child holds the light and you move; you hold the light and your child moves.

Exercise 4.
Balance, Balance

OBJECTIVE: To stimulate and develop equilibrium in the body.

WHEN TO DO: As with all exercises in this chapter, this one is important to do early in the program. It is particularly useful after outdoor playground time or even before, when children are ordinarily experiencing the control or loss of balance. Great also as a relaxation or focusing exercise, can be done impromptu right next to their seats.

DESCRIPTION: For groups or individuals: Have all children stand straight and tall, hands at their sides, feet together, insides of the legs touching. Now close the eyes and count, all together, 1–2–3–4 . . . all the way to ten. If anyone feels dizzy, they should open their eyes.

Now open the eyes, keep hands at sides, and bend one knee so that one foot is off the floor. Put the foot down, raise the arms like an airplane, extended to the side, and close the eyes. Everyone lower the arms, and open the eyes. Now repeat everything with the other knee bent.

Again, do not expect that this exercise can be accomplished immediately. Equilibrium or internal balance is not developed fully at this early age. It can develop gradually, each child at her own pace, through the repeated presentation of this activity.

◊ FUNDAMENTAL PLAYDANCES: AGES SIX TO EIGHT ◊

Exercise 1.
Touch Together

OBJECTIVE: To develop coordination while simultaneously heightening body awareness.

WHEN TO DO: A very good basic anatomy lesson. Fits nicely into "How the body works" section of most science curriculums.

DESCRIPTION: For groups or individuals: Have children arrange themselves in lines or in a large circle. The idea is for every child to have enough room to move around without bumping into somebody. Can they walk across the room keeping both hands on both knees? Is there only one way to do this?

Have them show you some other ways. Can they run, or hop, or jump and sit keeping their hands on their knees? What activities are more difficult? Why?

Now have them place their elbows on their knees and repeat the same instructions that you gave them when they had their hands on their knees. Is this position more or less difficult than the previous one? Why?

Continue in this way giving the children various combinations of body parts to explore: hand on head; elbow on hip; toe on ankle; knee on shoulder; etc. Once the children become comfortable exploring your instructions, have them volunteer some combinations of their own. In addition, have them establish what combinations are simple and why; what combinations are difficult and why; and what combinations are impossible—except perhaps for a contortionist.

Exercise 2.
Yoga

OBJECTIVE:	To develop flexibility and strength and awareness of how the body stretches and contracts.
WHEN TO DO:	Another good aid to a basic anatomy lesson or as part of a social studies curriculum in which you might explore practices of different cultures.
DESCRIPTION:	For groups or individuals: The illustrated positions are based upon yoga poses that relax and stretch all the most important muscles of the body. Since the poses presented are all pretty much geometric, it will be easy for you to see when a child is not preforming one correctly. Look at the poses pictured and practice them at home first. See which ones you are comfortable with.

RELAXATION

LOCUST
*Make two fists, place
under hip-bones to
support body.*

SHOULDER STAND
(PERISCOPE)
Arms support body.

BOW
Hands grasp ankles.

FISH
*Lift head and chest at
the same time.*

WHEEL
*Curve spine as evenly
as possible.*

PLOUGH
Hands flat on floor.

"SIT-DOWN" TWIST
*Turn to left, then
to right.*

POSTERIOR-STRETCHING
(FISHHOOK)
*Bring head to knees
if possible.*

POUNCING LION
*Arch spine. Complete
pose includes sticking
out tongue as far
toward chin as
possible.(!)*

COBRA
*Curve spine as
smoothly as possible.*

Yoga Poses

Make copies of these diagrams and show them to your students. Have everyone sit down on the floor (carpeting is preferable here but not absolutely necessary). The first time you present these exercises, demonstrate one at a time and have children rest between each pose. If a pose is easy for a child to do correctly, she should try to hold it for about 30 seconds. If a pose is really difficult (the Wheel and the Locust require a fair amount of strength), do not force. Omit it this time around. The repetition of certain exercises will eventually lead to greater ability.

When children are finished, ask them questions similar to those asked in Exercise 1: What exercises were most difficult? Most easy? Why? What exercise did they like doing the most? The least? Why?

Exercise 3.
Take a Good Look

OBJECTIVE: To establish the uniqueness of one's own body.

WHEN TO DO: Early in the Playdance program.

MATERIALS NEEDED: Polaroid camera and a video camera.

DESCRIPTION: For groups: Take individual Polaroids or make a videotape of the children in your class. You can take these pictures yourself or have someone else take them when the children are engaged in some standard classroom activities. Some children are apt to ham-it-up for the photographer, but do get pictures of children really doing something, not just posing. If you are going to make a video, as well as take photos, make sure all children are represented on the video. Once you have your pictures, divide the children into small groups with the pile of respective Polaroids in the center.

Everyone holds their own picture and several questions are asked. What are you doing in this picture and why are you doing it? Did you think you'd look like this when this picture was taken—

why or why not? Take a look at the picture of the person sitting to the right of you. How is what they were doing with their body different from what you were doing, and how is what you were doing the same? Okay, now take a look at the picture of the person on your left, and ask the same set of questions.

Either immediately or very soon after this activity, present your video. Review the questions you asked when the children were looking at their polaroids. In addition, now that they have seen the video, what do they know about how their bodies move that they did not know by just looking at the Polaroids?

The French mime, Etienne Decroux, once said that people walk as if they were children making faces in the dark: they think no one can see them. As Shrag indicated early in this chapter, how children move and use their bodies is intimately related to what and who they are. Giving children a window into themselves through movement is the first Playdancing experience.

◇ CHAPTER 6 ◇

Self-Awareness: Who Am I?

*The questions which one asks oneself begin to illuminate the world, and become
one's key to the experience of others*

JAMES BALDWIN, NOBODY KNOWS MY NAME

Walt Anderson, the psychiatrist, once remarked that one of his most
reassuring thoughts was that at any given moment, a sizable portion of
the human race was dancing—finding out who they were and
beginning to like themselves.[1] Paradoxically, one of the reasons dance
and its role in human development may have been trivialized is that it
feels so good right from the start. Self-discovery in our highly
verbalized, perhaps over-intellectualized society, should not be so
simple. It is supposed to be a long-enduring, even painful, learning
process. Yet the joy of dancing and the kind of self-exploration it
invokes may be one of the oldest forms of consciousness raising in
existence.

In Chapter Five, we explored the way in which the young child

[1]Anderson, Walter (1975). Pas de psyche. *Human Behavior*, 56–60.

discovers her body to develop a sense of self. But self-absorption and self-reflection are not the only skills on the road to creativity. Children must also learn to distinguish similarities and differences between themselves and others. They need to look outside their own bodies to take in information about how they fit into the world. This process of establishing relationships between oneself and the world is often referred to as self-awareness. It is a vital learning process as it helps children begin to see themselves as part of a greater whole. Much of children's understanding about how the world works is tied to their direct physical involvement, their feelings of competence, and the immediate appreciation of the moment itself.

One of the first important jobs teachers have in nurturing self-awareness is to discover how much children know about themselves in the dimensions of time and space. The child's first conscious discovery of dancing is how she relates to space and what movement means as travel in space.

Judy: Everyone, come with me in a high way,
in a low way.
a reaching way,
a creeping way,
a backwards way,
a sideways way,
a quick way,
a slow way.
Kyle: A flipping way,
a dipping way,
a slipping way,
a lapping way,
a clapping way.[Kyle stops moving but keeps chanting]
Judy: Kyle, what happened? How do you move in those ways?
Kyle: I don't know. That's why I stopped. I wanted to see what a clapping way looked like. See Louise, she's clapping!

When children compare sounds, seriate sounds, and translate these comparisons into creative movements in space, they are building their imagery system and their ability to transpose experiences from one sensory source to another. By using a drum and beating out a simple rhythm, Judy moved her class consciously into time and space, elements in which they have lived from birth, but seldom acknowledge or intentionally use.

How about the concept of moving versus not moving? It is extremely important for a teacher to clarify and ascertain that her class understands silence and stillness for what they are, since many children believe these to be a form of being dead, inert, or without thought and feeling. A knowledge of quiet and stillness naturally leads to an inquiry about self.

> *Morgan:* Listen; listen. Can you hear the leaves brushing against each other? Can you smell them in the air?
> *Peggie:* You know, I feel something new when I'm not moving around!

Almost always, children will, of their own volition, incorporate contrasts into their Playdances. These contrasts should be noted for them, so that they understand right from the beginning the importance of establishing differences. That is why lessons in movement and stillness, high and low, loud and soft, fast and slow, and the exercises that emerge from them provide a foundation for self-awareness.

The development of knowledge in the earliest stages of growth is personal. It depends upon the personal relationships between adult and child. The thinking of young children is also personally oriented. It is now accepted that the world of the child is a totality which often

The development of knowledge in the earliest stages of growth is personal. It depends upon the personal relationships between adult and child.

appears different from that in which the adult lives. The child who cries, "It doesn't wait for me" when she sees the water flowing away from her expresses this difference. This kind of perception of the world is also revealed in drawings of young children where the head or face is unusually large because it is the part that is important for the child.

In order for the child to understand her place in the world, she needs to understand what is truly special and unique about her. What, in essence, does she or can she contribute? What does she like to wear? Or what would she like to wear given a choice? What was she like when she was little? What is her favorite music? What does she like to eat? The questions and answers are endless and telling. In personalizing events for children, they come to understand the significance of individuality, and come to value diversity.

> *Linda:* Know what? Crosby is going to let us see his hearing aid today. But we have to be very careful. Hearing aids are special and not everyone can have one.
> *Torine:* Yeah, I know. I wanted a set of screw drivers real bad and mommie said I couldn't have a real set. They're special too and real expensive. But mommie bought me a toy set. Crosby, where can you buy toy hearing aides?
> *Crosby:* I don't know, but we could all make some.

Isadora Duncan once said that in her school she wouldn't teach children to imitate her movements, but to make their own—help them develop movements which were natural to them.[2] Yet in order to develop these natural movements, children need to appreciate something about themselves. By sharing his uniqueness with the class, Crosby began to understand how much like other children he really was. The "Crosby Dance" that followed his sharing reflected a new confidence and joy in all that was Crosby.

Fantasy and reality are often confused in children's thinking. What they think seems true to them whether it corresponds to reality or not. Children need help and time to make this distinction between reality and fantasy, without having to reject their fantasy. They have a right to imagine and create fantasies as well as a need to learn reality. Hence, the value of dramatic play in Playdancing. Here, children can expand self-concepts by developing dancing roles. Costumes, makeup, and props can aid in the development of characters otherwise dormant in the child.

---

[2]Duncan, Isadora. *My Life.* Garden City, NY: Garden City Publishing Company, 1927.

Steve: Oh, that's my old graduation robe. You can use it if you like.
Amanda: I am! I am . . . the wizard; the wizard!
Steve: Whose voice is that? I never heard you talk like that.
Amanda: I never had the magic robe.

The growth and development of creativity in each child is an individual occurrence. The process and outcome of this growth stems from innumerable individual opportunities for creative experiences. Some of these experiences produce learning which is universal to most children and is acquired in a similar fashion, while some learning is unique to the individual child. The following sets of Playdances address this latter learning process: that of discovering and defining the uniqueness of self.

◇ THE DEVELOPMENT OF SELF-AWARENESS: AGES THREE TO FIVE ◇

The "hatching process" which occurs at about four to five months of age normally indicates the first subphase of separation/individuation. Separation and individuation are two distinct but complementary processes. Separation involves the child's initial emergence from a stage in which she is physically and emotionally fused with the mother. Individuation marks the child's first awareness of her own unique characteristics. The preferential smiling for mother is the crucial sign that the infant has recognized herself and her special relationship with another. This process, though evidenced early, is lifelong, and very much bound to the development of body image and self-esteem. The young preschool child normally evolves through several self-awareness phases.

1. Self-constancy. The concept that the self is permanent. For example, when I fall asleep, I will wake up and be relatively the same as I was yesterday.
2. Self-differentiation. The concept that one's ideas are one's own and not necessarily held by others. For example, I like chocolate cake, but Susie likes ice cream better.
3. Self-identity. The ideas surrounding uniqueness. For example, I like riding tricycles real slow and wearing a new red skirt to bed.
4. Self-esteem. The concept that one and one's behavior is acceptable and valued.

All of these concepts are felt first by feeling them in the body. We know *that we are, who we are,* and that *we like ourselves* because of physical feelings. If a young child cannot or will not experience feelings physically, then they cannot conceptualize these feelings. All of the following Playdances promote these emerging self-awareness concepts.

◊ SELF-AWARENESS PLAYDANCES: AGES THREE TO FIVE ◊

Exercise 1.
Can You Come With Me?

OBJECTIVE: To foster self-constancy and self-differentiation.

WHEN TO DO: In conjunction with any self-awareness or self-esteem curriculum. Also, although not presented in the following chapter as a language activity, can certainly be used as such to explore adjectives, verbs, etc.

MATERIALS NEEDED: A small drum.

DESCRIPTION: For groups or individuals: Begin to beat a clear definitive rhythm on your drum, preferably in 4/4 time. This is an instant attention-getter. Once children gather together in follow-the-leader fashion, begin a series of chanting phrases: Can you come with me in a *high* way, a *low* way.

Go slowly, giving children time to explore, then change directions, keeping a steady rhythm. You can present contrasts: a quick way; a slow way; a forward way; and a backward way. Or you can present a series of rhymes: a go way; a no way; a top way; and a stop way.

Ask the children for suggestions. When they are comfortable with concrete directions like up and down, slow and fast, help them develop more imaginative phrases like: a rocking way; a knocking way; or a locking way. Children can be divided into

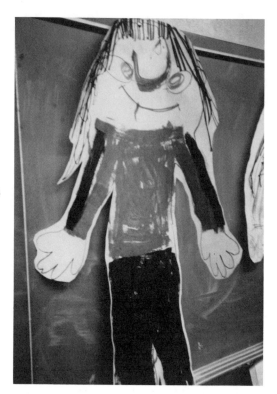

Exercise: Tracings

smaller groups to develop their own series of ways, with one child as the leader using the drum.

Exercise 2.
Tracings

OBJECTIVE: To develop self-constancy, self-differentiation, and self-identity.

WHEN TO DO: In conjunction with any self-awareness curriculum. Also excellent as a language expression activity as it does have a significant narrative or storytelling portion.

MATERIALS NEEDED: Large roll of craft paper, markers, crayons, paint, yarn, material scraps, buttons, tape, paste, and glue.

DESCRIPTION: For groups: Stretch out sheets of craft paper and tape each one securely to the floor. Have all children lie

a folder. You can tell the children that everyone is a baby for a short time. We forget most of what happens to us when we are babies but most of the time people tell us things we did or said at the time. Does anyone have a baby story to tell? As children relay their baby stories, have them look at their pictures as well. What kind of baby do they think they were? Did they run around? How do babies walk, or crawl? How do they eat when they sit in their highchair?

Each child should be encouraged to make a baby dance either alone or in a group. Again, after each baby dance, children should be encouraged to explain, however briefly, why they moved the way they did.

Baby pictures should be displayed for all to see. Storybooks can be placed in the book corner for children to leaf through, and individual pictures can simply be mounted on the bulletin board. Children should be given the opportunity to see how unique and special they are, and that they were that way right from the beginning.

For individuals: Here perhaps the best alternative is to have your child make her own baby book. This could take a while, but children should be encouraged to use as many pictures as they like. Then you can sit together the first several times while you narrate the story behind the pictures. After a few sessions, your child should be able to discuss some of the pictures with you, reviewing stories you have told. She can also make up her own stories if she is so inclined. Baby dances can be constructed in pretty much the same say they were for the group, having her explore baby-like movements that reflect what she feels she was like when she was a baby.

Exercise 5.
Moving in Space

OBJECTIVE: To foster self-differentiation and self-identity.

WHEN TO DO: As part of any self-awareness curriculum. Also, a good pre-math activity to explore dimension.

A great companion to the ever popular Three Bears story.

MATERIALS
NEEDED:
Different size cardboard boxes, empty shelves, bolsters, and expanding tunnels.

DESCRIPTION:
For groups: Point out that the world is full of space. Spaces can be very, very big or very, very small. The world is also full of people and things big and small. Some people and things fit more easily into some spaces than others. If you have your shelves empty and they are absolutely safety-proof, no nails or sharp edges, you can start here. Have the children begin to explore the different spaces and corners in the room. What spaces are an easy fit, and what ones are harder? After they are satisfied, you can have the children help you set up a kind of space maze with cartons, bolsters, and tunnels. Every child should be encouraged to explore as many spaces as possible.

For individuals: This activity does warrant a child-proof place but basically can be performed in a manner very similar to that presented to a group.

Exercise 6.
Body Prints

OBJECTIVE:
To develop self-constancy, self-differentiation, and self-identity.

WHEN TO DO:
As part of any self-awareness curriculum.

MATERIALS
NEEDED:
Large roll of craft paper, paint, and paint trays.

DESCRIPTION:
For groups: Tape several large sheets of craft paper to the floor or walls. Children should be wearing smock-type clothes (the kind that if they poured paint all over them, it wouldn't matter). Roll up sleeves and pant legs. Filled paint trays can be spread about the room so that two to three children are using any one sheet of craft paper. Children can begin by dipping their hands either individually or together into the paint and then pressing their imprints onto the

paper. They can use the back or front of the hands or the fingertips. Feet, elbows, and knees should be explored in a similar fashion until a huge collage of body prints appears on the walls and floors. After the body print collage is dry, children should be encouraged to reflect upon the differences and similarities in the body prints. Some children may have small feet, large hands, long toes, etc. Yet children are also very similar to one another. Differences are important because they help us know who we are, yet it is also important to know how alike we are so we know when and how to help each other.

For individuals: Paint-proofing your home will certainly be a consideration when choosing to do this exercise, yet the actual presentation of materials and ideas should be pretty much the same as it was for the group.

Exercise: Costume

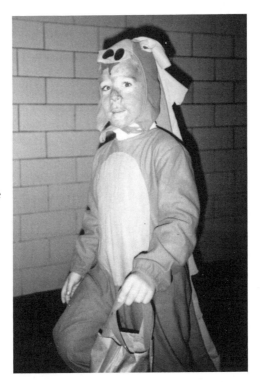

Exercise 7.
Costume

OBJECTIVE: To expand self-identify through dramatic play.

WHEN TO DO: Costuming and/or dress-up is an important component of dramatic play. Can also be utilized in conjunction with a social studies format which focuses on the customs or dress of other cultures or on the role of community helpers such as policemen, teachers, doctors, dentists, etc.

MATERIALS NEEDED: Various clothing and costume pieces (masks are not advisable for three- to five-year-olds), make-up, and props such as handbags, or wands.

DESCRIPTION: For groups: A good costume collection may take a while to adequately develop. A notice home to parents is recommended as they are almost always a good resource for dress-up materials. Suitable items are hats, shoes, ties, bags, or any clothing that is easily put on and removed. Sheets of materials that can be roped and tied into just about anything are good, and uniforms are great for young children because identifying with specific roles is important. It is also advisable to haunt the local thrift store and the Five and Dime during Halloween to find colorful jewelry, capes, and crowns. Children should be encouraged to create a costume or series of dress-up pieces and then create a dance about the person, animal, or even thing (monster, etc.) that they are depicting. Children can do solos, duets, or even small group dances. Accompaniment can be small percussive instruments or taped music. Younger children may be more comfortable depicting someone or something with which they have had an actual experience (a dog, their mommy, or a frog), but princesses and vampires can also be represented. Older children are more likely to display the fantastic: marshmallow snowman, or star-fighters, particularly considering the influence of the media. Older children might also have fun exploring the interaction between two opposite persons such as a princess and a witch, a devil and an angel, or a bird and a fish.

For individuals: When you are working with a single child, it is easier to personalize costumes, spending time on detail and make-up. You may want to devise your own costume to encourage dramatic interplay.

Exercise 8.
My Favorite Things

OBJECTIVE: To foster self-identity and self-esteem.

WHEN TO DO: As part of any self-awareness curriculum. Also effective as a language arts activity.

MATERIALS NEEDED: Shoe boxes and construction paper.

DESCRIPTION: For groups or individuals: Have children bring in either pictures of favorite things or the actual favorites from home. You can assist in this process by salvaging your own magazine treasures and having children flip through these for favorites. If children have selected pictures, have them assembled in a construction paper book for easy presentation. Children who have brought in actual objects should place them in an shoebox. Some children will opt to have both a book and a box. Each has an advantage. Pictures allow for things you cannot fit in a shoebox and a box allows you to keep the real things on hand.

This activity can be presented innumerable times throughout the school year as children assume new and perhaps even discard old favorites. You can introduce the activity yourself or, as children get the hang of it, have them initiate it during the week. Children select an item, tell about who gave it to them or where they found it, why they like it, and how it makes them feel. Most Show and Tell's end here, not allowing children to show their ideas or feelings about their special thing. Here children should be encouraged to either move like the object itself (for example, a ball, a robot) or move the way it makes them feel. The younger the child the more easy it will be for them to simply imitate the object. But the older preschooler and kindergartener should be able to give you some physical insights into feelings.

Exercise 9.
Textures

OBJECTIVE: To foster self-differentiation and self-identity. Note: This exercise is easily adapted for the six-to eight-year-old.

WHEN TO DO: As part of any self-awareness curriculum. Also effective as a language arts activity because verbal description is central, or as a science activity in which aspects of physical matter are being explored.

MATERIALS NEEDED: Boxful of differently textured materials: silk, sandpaper, cotton balls, jars of water, glue, sand, stuffed toys, rubber bands—virtually anything that has a distinctive feel to it. Cartons or shoe boxes.

DESCRIPTION: For groups or individuals: Distribute collected materials into several cartons or shoe boxes, and have the children begin to explore these with their hands. Blindfolds can be used to help some children focus upon the experience of feeling, but many children can simply be told to close their eyes once they have discovered an interesting texture. They should explore their chosen materials for at least twenty seconds before you begin questioning: What other things feel like what you have in your hand? What things would feel very different, or the opposite? How does this thing make you feel: glad, happy, sleepy, prickly, sticky? And if you were sticky (happy, sleepy, etc.), how would you move? Have each child experience different ways that they can move to appear glad or prickly. As with earlier Playdance activities, children can elect to do solos, duets, or small group dances. Children should be encouraged to explore as many materials as possible, comparing and contrasting the differences in texture.

◇ THE DEVELOPMENT OF SELF-AWARENESS: AGES SIX TO EIGHT ◇

For children this age, self-awareness concepts of self-constancy, self-differentiation, self-identity, and self-esteem are expanded to include evaluation of these concepts. The older school-age child is equipped with a vivid imagination and an ability to abstract that is not yet developed in the preschooler. They can judge creative experiences and choose to include or discard ideas. They can also monitor the development and rehearsal of a specific Playdance, narrate stories, and assign roles.

Even though later Playdances may be subject to more scrutiny than earlier ones, it is important for teachers to understand that all movement expression, although carefully disguised in a piece of music or a fanciful prop is essentially self-mirroring. All dances reflect parts of the self. This is why movement is so significant. Here the extremely verbal school-age child can express feelings and desires that she may feel uncomfortable talking about.

◇ SELF-AWARENESS PLAYDANCES: AGES SIX TO EIGHT ◇

Exercise 1.
How could you . . . ?

OBJECTIVE: To expand self-identity.

WHEN TO DO: As part of any self-awareness curriculum.

DESCRIPTION: For groups or individuals: This activity is essentially a series of puzzles to solve using the body in one way, but not another. A series of questions is posed and various solutions are presented. How could you get across that carpet without using your feet? Pick up that spoon without using your hands? Put on that hat without using your arms? Climb those stairs without using your knees?

The solutions to those four questions alone are endless. Again, this exercise becomes more finely tuned with repetition. Once children are comfortable with this exercise they can begin developing and posing their own questions. As always, children should be given the time to reflect upon the many solutions to a single problem.

Exercise 2.
Space Patterns

OBJECTIVE:	To foster self-differentiation and self-identity.
WHEN TO DO:	As part of any self-awareness curriculum.
MATERIALS NEEDED:	Sheets of blank paper.
DESCRIPTION:	For groups: Have each child draw some simple line designs on a blank sheet of paper. Now ask them how they could recreate these designs using their bodies in space. Designs can be taped to the wall or the floor. Initial movements may simply involve walking, hopping, or sliding the pattern out on the floor, or drawing it in the air with a hand or foot. Duets can be formed as partners walk out different pieces of the same pattern. By dividing children into small groups, one child can move other children's bodies into shapes that mimic a given pattern.

As always, children should try to create as many different types of designs as possible: ones with straight lines, ones with curved. Discussions can involve the ease or complexity with which given patterns are performed. Was it easier for you to make curved or straight shapes? Why?

For individuals: Although you will not have the multiple bodies to form complex designs, individual children can easily maneuver their drawn patterns by walking, hopping, slipping, or sliding on the floor. Simple patterns can be formed by individual bodies, and you, of course, can join in.

Exercise 3.
Weather Report

OBJECTIVE:	To foster self-identity.
WHEN TO DO:	As part of any self-awareness curriculum. Also interesting as part of a language arts program, or when discussing the change of seasons.
DESCRIPTION:	For groups or individuals: Have children clip weather reports from the newspaper. Some children may be able to read these themselves while others may still be in the reading acquisition stage. It may be helpful simply to read some of the collected reports aloud to the class.

Weather: today, partly sunny, windy and cold.
tomorrow, cloudy, chance of rain.

Now, how could you be sunny with your body? or windy? or cloudy? or cold? How could you be thunder or lightning or rain? Could you be very, very hot? How do you move when you are hot? or cold? or when it's pouring?

Once children have explored various weather components, see if they can piece together an original weather report, either individually or with several children. Write the reports down in clear legible writing and tape them on the wall or floor. Solos, duets, or small groups can set movements together exploring different elements of their own reports. Children can also be asked to exchange reports and create Playdances from reports they did not write themselves. Children can elect to be accompanied by a drum, some small percussive instruments, or with an actual piece of music. Children can also move accompanying themselves with vocalizations or clapping and stomping to represent environmental sounds.

Exercise: Human
Emotion

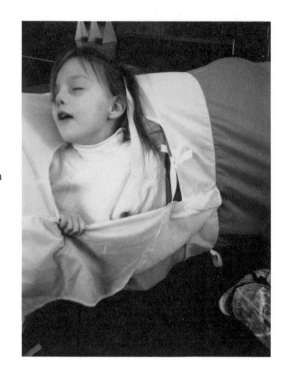

Exercise 4.
Human Emotion

OBJECTIVE: To foster self-identify and self-esteem.

WHEN TO DO: As part of any self-awareness curriculum. Also effective in conjunction with a social studies curriculum in which you would explore the native dances of different peoples. Most native dances are functional and support the expression of specific feelings.

MATERIALS NEEDED: Various musical selections.

DESCRIPTION: For individuals: The beauty in working with one child in this activity is the degree of involvement that you can have in the discussion of individual emotions. If a child is fascinated by anger, you can really spend some time talking about it and moving!

For groups: It is very important for children to understand that feelings or emotions serve a purpose. No feeling should be thought of as inherently good or bad. Sometimes it is just as important to be angry or sad as it is to be happy or joyful. A good way to begin is to dim the lights and have children lie down on their backs. Put on a music selection that is light and airy. *Waltz of the Flowers* is a good example. Have them listen for a few minutes, then turn the lights back on and have them sit up.

Discussion can involve what kinds of pictures they made in their heads while the music was playing. Once children have clarified their ideas, dim the lights once again. This time tell children to put these pictures into their bodies and to move the way the music makes them feel.

Suggested Music for Specific Emotional Content:

Emotion	Composer	Piece
Happy/Joyful	Gershwin	*An American in Paris*
	Handel	*Messiah*
	Mendelssohn	*A Midsummer's Night Dream*
	Mozart	*German Dances*
	Sousa	*Washington Post March*
	Tschaikowsky	*Waltz of the Flowers*
Anger	Chopin	*Polonaise: Ab Major, Etude in Gb Major*
	Dukas	*The Sorcerer's Apprentice*
	Rachmaninoff	*Concerto no. 1*
	Wagner	*Die Walkure*
Fear	Holst	*The Planets: Mars, Bringer of War*
	Moussorgsky	*Night on Bald Mountain*
	Tibetan Chant	*Lament for the Dead*
Sadness	Brahms	*Piano Concerto no.2 (2nd Movement)*
	Debussy	*Beau Soir* *Three Nocturnes*
	Ravel	*Le Tombeau de cauperin*
	Wagner	*Tristan and Isolde: Liebestad*
Excitement	Berlioz	*Symphonie Phantastique*
	DeFalla	*Ritual Fire Dance*
	Stravinsky	*Firebird Suite*

This list is by no means exhaustive or absolute. Once children become familiar with exploring various emotional content in music, they can start adding to the collection themselves. Through experiencing feelings in a conscious, direct manner, children can begin to see how similar or different the various emotions are. Joy or ecstasy feels very similar to excitement, yet it is also close to anger. There are also feelings not on the previous list that are certainly worthy of investigation: jealously, serenity, anxiety, etc. All of these can be explored as well.

Young children's experience of the world is at once cognitive, aesthetic, psychomotor, and social. Their entire attention is focused upon solving a problem in the service of self-discovery. They stand ready to explore again and again, until they feel satisfied and supported in their discovery. Each child needs a different amount of time to discover and replenish her own sense of self-worth. All tasks can be seen as elements in this self-discovery process whether it be tying a shoe, riding a tricycle, pouring some juice, writing one's name, or jumping very high. In each case the child's sense of personal value resides in her feelings about her own physical self. Once this strong body image and self-concept are addressed, the child is ready to reach out and communicate feelings about herself and her world. It is only through self-discovery and understanding that creativity can blossom.

◇ *CHAPTER 7* ◇

Language:
How Do I Tell You How I Feel?

There comes about a separation between the life of movement and the life of thought. Since the child has a body as well as a mind, we feel we must include games in his curriculum, so as to avoid neglecting any part of nature's provisions. But to be always thinking of the mind, on one hand, and the body, on the other, is to break the continuity that reigns between them

MARIA MONTESSORI, THE ABSORBENT MIND

The experience of self is bound up intrinsically with language and communication. One can never understand perfectly the inside of another's experience, and so we have words. But words do not tell all. In fact, without the body and its many communication cues including eye gaze, gesture, and tone of voice, speech alone is very difficult to understand. It is the difference between talking on the phone to someone as opposed to speaking with them directly. As Virginia Satir so eloquently phrased, "Nonverbal behavior is an elaborate code that is written nowhere, known by none, and understood by all."[1] We

[1]Satir, Virginia. *Conjoint Family Therapy.* Palo Alto, CA: Science and Behavior Books, 1967.

cannot separate the verbal from the nonverbal experience anymore than we can separate the body from the mind and why should we want to? Total communication is dependent upon them working together.

In an era when electronic information is at one's fingertips, when satellites bring the world's wonders and excitement into our living rooms, you might ask why concern ourselves with language and communication? Answered simply, the initial reasons are to reassure, to entertain, to inform, to explain, to arouse curiosity, and to inspire—and to do it all personally, not impersonally with a machine. All those experiences create and strengthen a child's sense of self, and this self-concept, as discussed in Chapter Six, is the foundation stone upon which you build learning appetites.

Secondly, teachers and parents are unaware of their role as a prime model in children's language development. They would both do well to take a tip from Madison Avenue. We have a product to sell. When the U.S. Department of Education is telling us that one in five Americans cannot decipher the directions on a can of soup, it is perhaps time for adults to sell an important product: language.

Finally, few tasks present children with as monumental a challenge, and few tasks are as far reaching in their consequences, as the challenge of learning to communicate. The ability to communicate effectively affects our ability to read and write, to understand ideas and relationships, and to succeed in a chosen career. We simply cannot function in our society without being able to communicate, and communicate well! As Americans move from a manufacturing toward an information society, the need to be articulate becomes essential, rather than superfluous, in determining an individual's ultimate success in the contemporary world. Yet adults and children often have problems communicating with each other:

> *Tim:* "Nobody don't want this."
> *Angela:* "No; say nobody wants this."
> *Tim:* "Nobody don't want this."
> *Angela:* "No; now listen carefully; say nobody wants this."
> *Tim:* "Oh, nobody don't wants this."
> *Angela:* "No, no. You're not listening!"

As I have reiterated throughout this text, children often see their world very differently from adults. Adults assume this is because children do not see the world the way "it really is." In a trivial sense that is true. But children know and feel many things. Their thoughts might be strange in an adult, *but they are right for kids*. How does it all feel from the child's perspective? Take Tim, for instance. Angela wants Tim to say "wants," and Tim is saying "wants." Why is Angela getting upset? Until Angela is able to take Tim's perspective, she will have difficulty communicating her need for him to speak in grammatically correct sentences.

The world and pattern of children's earliest efforts in language and communication permits adults to take a peek into a remarkable world, barely beyond memory. Children's language reveals a great deal about how people learn, how people motivate themselves, how people create, and more. Educators and clinicians might have people believe that the true value of language learning is the boost it gives to the intellect. Important as these intellectual goals are, there are other reasons for being concerned by how children communicate. Young children exhibit a vivacity in communicating and learning that can serve as a model for all of us.

Children's language has attracted widespread attention of late, and recent research has brought startling new advances in what we now know about children's language. First, language is a lot to learn. Imagine how you would feel if you found yourself in some strange culture where everybody spoke a language you did not understand. You would be overwhelmed by the enormity of what you would have to learn in order to communicate. Yet this is exactly what all young children need to succeed in learning long before kindergarten.

Secondly, children are not small adults. Most of us have a bundle of stereotyped assumptions about children's talking we routinely use, and not always wisely. Few adults stop to think about how they talk to children since they rarely hear adults talking to children in other ways. We need to assume that children are different, and very different in the ways they choose to express themselves from any stereotype we might hold of them.

A third point to consider is that the young child's verbalizations, whether audible to others or just inner speech, exerts a strong regulatory function on learning and behavior. By the time a child enters kindergarten, self-generated instructions help problem-solving just as often as adult intervention.

Like any other complex task, using language effectively requires creative thinking. When you think creatively, you are generally perceiving and translating several pieces of information. For example, suppose you are reading a story about a balloon-man to your class. Even though there may be an actual picture of a balloon-man in this book, every child is still likely to create her own mental picture of a balloon-man. In addition, she will hear what this balloon-man says as you are reading the story and create her own balloon-man voice. As she is seeing and hearing this balloon-man in her imagination, she may also be deciding what kinds of feelings she has for the man. Each child's seeing and hearing and feeling are all occurring at a rapid-fire pace in her imagination so that within a few minutes of beginning this balloon-man story, each child has integrated enough information to create her own interpretation of what a balloon-man is. The process of creative thinking itself is closely related to the process of integrating information, which is an essential component of critical thinking.

As you continue your story, each child will also use her imagination to organize her thoughts into logical patterns. This sequencing and organizing of information are as essential to the creative process as the integration of that information. The relationship between the creative process and language integration and organizational skills is like a loaf of bread and its ingredients. Depending upon the type of bread you are baking, you will normally use certain ingredients such as flour, eggs, butter, and yeast. But what if you do not combine these ingredients together but instead bake each ingredient separately? Or if you bake the same loaf of bread but reverse two ingredients, putting the eggs in before the yeast? Though the contents of your recipe will still be the same, your products will be decidedly different.

Such is the case with creativity. Even though a child may have the necessary language skills to be able to communicate effectively, she needs to be channeled to expand and reflect on these abilities. The manner in which language concepts are integrated and organized will differ for every child. Yet it is precisely here that most language activities in the classroom are observed to end. Teachers of three- to five-year-olds read the story, ask a few questions, and put the book away. Teachers of six- to eight-year-olds behave similarly, only they have the children read the story. They ask a few questions, and the books are put away.

So how can creative movement be used to enhance the child's imagination in language? A number of recent studies have indicated that the imaginative, integrative, and organizational skills related to language can be enhanced by building language concepts into the structure of symbolic play and creative movement activities. Both these activities are often referred to as "language experience exercises." In language experience exercises, the young child uses various learning materials to act out her own version of a familiar story or concept, or one she has made up herself. In this way, the art of expressive and rhythmic body movement can be effectively utilized to enhance a variety of language skills.

The Playdances in this chapter prepare children for language comprehension by teaching them to use their imaginations for both integrating and organizing language information. Each activity is organized to include the materials needed for the activity and the optimal time to present the activity. Playdances have been designed in many instances to reflect commonplace activities in the early childhood language arts curriculum (for example, "letter learning," "nursery rhymes," and "the book report") and are readily available to implement in most any early childhood program. Obviously, the objective for all the Playdances in this section is to stimulate the use of creative language.

◇ THE LANGUAGE DEVELOPMENT PROCESS: AGES THREE TO FIVE ◇

The process of children's language development is the topic of many exceptional texts. One cannot hope to do justice to this area of development within a chapter except in a very preliminary way. However, in order to implement Playdancing effectively, one needs a basic understanding of the language development process. (See additional reading in the Selected Bibliography and the Developmental Chart in Chapter Three.)

Between ages three and five, children's sentences become longer and more complex. Children begin to elaborate the way they say things by adding more detail. They fill in words and word endings that were missing in their earliest utterances. For the first time, they begin to use articles, prepositions, pronouns, auxiliary verbs like "is" and "are," plurals, and the past tense. Their vocabulary continues to grow and they use many new words.

Children learn more complex ways to use language socially and begin to develop discourse skills such as participating in discussions, giving instructions, and providing descriptions about objects, events, and people. Children progress from talking about the here and now to talking about the there and then. They talk about past and future events and about objects and events in the absence of these props. In addition, particularly during the kindergarten year and even earlier, children begin a fascination with the world of words and reading. All of the aforementioned skills are supported by the Playdances that follow. Careful inspection of these Playdances will allow you to select what activities your children are ready for and what ones parallel the aims of your language arts curriculum.

◇ LANGUAGE PLAYDANCES: AGES THREE TO FIVE ◇

Exercise 1.
The Balloon-Man

OBJECTIVE: To develop and enhance creative use of language. Also assists in language comprehension.

WHEN TO DO: During any story time activity.

MATERIALS NEEDED: Any children's story, paper, and assorted art materials.

DESCRIPTION: For groups and individuals: Select a story the children are familiar with, or better yet, have them select one. Read the story as you ordinarily would, then ask the children to decide which one of the characters they each like best. You choose a favorite character for yourself as well. If there are pictures of these characters in the book, examine them together. Now tell the children that you are going to make your own "balloon-men" (or whatever characters you have selected). Have them individually select the art materials they want to use (these could include paint, marking pens, and collage materials) and assemble these materials. Now make your "balloon-men." Take your time. In some cases, this exercise will not be finished in one sitting. Once the balloon-men are finished, sit down together with the children and talk about the balloon-men. Ask them some open-ended questions, for example, why did you choose those colors? Or, how did you pin the legs on that way? After you have finished exploring your creations together, ask each child how she thinks her balloon-man would move. For example, if the balloon-man could walk, how would it walk? Or, if it could roll, how would it roll?, etc. After she has demonstrated several balloon-man movements, have her chain these movements together to make her own balloon-man dance.

This activity can also be done by selecting one character for all children to create. The focus here would be to demonstrate how different each created balloon-man could be from the others. Whatever you choose, every child should be given as long as she needs to make her balloon-man, talk about her balloon-man, and make her balloon-man dance. Certain children are much more hesitant and reflective than others. They should not be regarded as slow.

Again, this activity, if done with a large group, could take five or six sessions. The Balloon-Man Playdance is applicable to almost any children's story and should be utilized often.

Exercise 2.
Musical Pictures

OBJECTIVE: To develop and enhance creative use of language. Also helps children transpose information from one sensory source to another—an important skill for reading acquisition.

WHEN TO DO: During any music activity.

MATERIALS NEEDED: Musical selection, brown craft paper, and assorted art materials.

DESCRIPTION: For groups and individuals: Have a child select a favorite piece of music. An instrumental selection is preferred as it is more abstract, yet if she insists on *Sesame Street* tunes, this is perfectly all right. Tape a large sheet of brown craft paper to the floor for all the children. Tell the children you are going to "paint some music together," and assemble some assorted art materials. As you play the music, ask the children to think of the colors, lines, and images that the music makes them feel and to draw these on the craft paper. If you are using paint as opposed to markers or crayons, which can also be used, you may need to allow time for the picture to dry after the music is finished. If not, you can hang the picture on the wall immediately after it is completed.

Sit back, away from the picture, and begin to talk about it with the children. What did this music make them think about? Or, Why did it make you so sad? (happy, scared, etc.). Again, what you are trying to accomplish here is for each child to reflect on her thinking and begin to use language in ways she might not on her own. Now put the music back on again. This time the children are going to dance the way this music and drawing have made them feel. You can either dance each of the dances separately, in small clusters, or in one large group.

This exercise should be experienced so that each child can avail herself of the opportunity to make her own musical selection. Obviously, then, this exercise can be repeated many times. The child making a selection should discuss it with the group and teacher in an open forum beforehand. The teacher does not have to tape the paper to the floor. The teacher can tape it across the four walls of the room or have each child work on her own individual musical picture. Regardless of method, adequate time should be given for individual reflection on both the process of converting the sounds of music into pictures and the process of converting both into movement.

Exercise 3.
Nursery Rhymes

OBJECTIVE: To develop and enhance creative use of language. Also assists in language comprehension.

WHEN TO DO: When a child or group of children shows an interest in nursery rhymes, either by singing one out loud or bringing in a nursery rhyme book, etc.

MATERIALS NEEDED: A book of nursery rhymes.

DESCRIPTION:	For groups and individuals: Children love nursery rhymes. If they did not, they couldn't have remained as popular as they have for so very long. Most children know them by heart before they have any real comprehension of what they mean. Sit down with the children and your nursery rhyme book. Ask a child to pick out one or two she likes the most. When she has made her selection, ask her why she chose these particular ones. See if she can recite the chosen rhymes back to you. Most children can.

Many nursery rhymes are filled with opportunities for spontaneous creative movement. "Jack and Jill," for example, has all that climbing and rolling and falling. "Jack be Nimble" has that wonderful leap over the candlestick. Choose a nursery rhyme for yourself, one that the child did not select. Demonstrate for the children how you can say and dance the nursery rhyme simultaneously. Now ask several children to do the same.

Children may have difficulty coordinating both the language and movement aspects together but that is the challenge! They may need to rehearse their dance several times before they are happy with it. Be patient and allow these rehearsals.

Again, make sure you reflect on this activity subsequently, asking specific children which nursery rhymes they preferred and why they liked them, etc. Also, a teacher might opt for a cluster of children to work on a single nursery rhyme, each child working on a particular character.

Exercise 4.
Talking Tapes

OBJECTIVE:	To develop and enhance creative use of language. Also assists in language development.
WHEN TO DO:	During any discussion activity, such as "circle time."
MATERIALS NEEDED:	Tape recorders and tape cassettes.

For groups and individuals: "Talking tapes" is very adaptable to groups provided you have access to more than one tape recorder and pair of hands. Tape recorders and other electronic or media equipment are particularly fascinating to this age group, so it will be difficult for children to wait their turn if there is only one tape recorder. You might want to divide the group into small clusters, each with his own tape recorder.

Explain and demonstrate the use of a tape recorder to your children. Ask a child, in turn, to say something such as her name, and then immediately play it back. Ask her to tell a little story about herself, what she did this morning. Young children are fascinated by hearing their voices on a tape recorder and generally will be highly motivated to keep such an activity going. When she has finished the story, ask her if she could make a little Playdance go along with the story. When she indicates she is finished, replay the story while she dances simultaneously.

This activity is particularly good for young children who may not be natural talkers. If used properly, this activity can encourage the more reserved child to open up and start producing more language. When she has finished her Playdance, ask her to talk about it, what she liked about it, and what other stories she would like to tell.

If the children are older, four-and-a-half or five, one child may be able to tell the story, and the others make the Playdance. If they are younger, it will still be very important for each child to have his own turn. Each tape talking Playdance can then be presented to a larger group, each storyteller being given an opportunity to reflect upon and expand his story, if he chooses. This is a wonderful language activity for young children as it gives them the feedback of their own voices and the physical experience of interpreting their voices. Rarely are young children given the opportunity to hear themselves. Remember, this Playdance, like many others, should be done often.

Exercise 5.
Rhyming Rhythms

OBJECTIVE: To develop and enhance creative use of language. Also a good language comprehension activity.

WHEN TO DO: When a child or children show an interest in rhyming.

DESCRIPTION: For groups and individuals: Tell the children that you are going to play a rhyming game with them. Explain that rhyming words are those words that sound alike, like the words "fat," "rat," and "pat." Have the children repeat these words back to you.

Now ask if anyone can show you with their body what the word "fat" looks like. Maybe they can pretend to be a balloon and blow up. How about the word "rat"? Can they move like a rat crawling on the floor? How about the word "pat"? Can they pat themselves like clay into a flat pancake. When they have completed the first three words, ask for other rhyming words to add to the list, for example, "sat," "bat," and "mat."

Children should be encouraged to develop other rhyming lists for other rhyming game times. Suggestions might include: "man," "ran," and "fan." "Beat," "feat," and "seat." "Spoon," "noon," and "tune."

Keep packs of index cards with different rhyming lists for the future.

Exercise 6.
Letter Learning

OBJECTIVE: To aid in letter recognition.

WHEN TO DO: When children demonstrate interest in print and letters; a great activity for any pre-reading curriculum.

MATERIALS NEEDED: Flashcards with lower case letters printed on them. Chalk and chalk board or marking pen with sheets of craft paper.

Exercise: Letter Learning

DESCRIPTION: For groups and individuals: Preparation will involve printing enough lower case letters for each member of your class. Decide upon four or five letters to begin with and hand out individual printed letters to each child. Most reading programs emphasize lower case letters now as opposed to capitals, but there is no problem presenting upper and lower case letters together. Depending upon the pre-reading program you are presently using, letters can be presented in standard alphabetical order, just vowels, or letters that look alike, like lower case "b," "d," and "p." Whatever your decision, it should complement your readiness program.

Either with chalk or marking pen, make a large letter on the board or on craft paper. While saying the name of the letter, have the children trace the letter with the index finger of their preferred hand. Can they make the shape of this letter using their whole body? Encourage them to experiment making the same letter in different positions, such as lying down, kneeling, or standing on tiptoe. Repeat this procedure using the four or five letters you have printed.

After presenting each of the prepared letters, ask children what letters were easier to make with their bodies, the hardest, the most fun, etc. This exercise will take many sessions to complete if you plan to incorporate the entire alphabet.

Exercise 7.
The Picture Box

OBJECTIVE: To develop and enhance creative use of language. Also encourages language development.

WHEN TO DO: Should be firmly integrated into any language arts curriculum—a mainstay!

MATERIALS NEEDED: Colorfully decorated cartons, old magazines, and picture books (those that are worn enough to be cut apart).

DESCRIPTION: For groups: Bring in several medium-sized food cartons from the supermarket. You can divide children into small clusters to decorate them. Children can cut and paste collage-style or draw with crayons and markers. When finished, each should be clearly labeled "the picture box."

Each week, children should be encouraged to look through old magazines and coloring or picture books to select preferred pictures. Children can also bring in pictures from home. These pictures should be placed in one of the decorated picture boxes. At the end of the week, or whenever is deemed appropriate, children can pick a picture from one of the boxes.

Each child should have a turn to talk about her picture. Ask her what she thinks is happening in the picture. Have her develop a little story about the picture. How about a dance to go with the picture? Children can also be asked to respond to an individual picture as a group. The beauty of movement is that all can respond with dance simultaneously, without interrupting each other. This exercise is meant to be done again and again, each week adding new pictures to the picture box.

For individuals: If you are working with an

individual child, you can opt to look through magazines and coloring books together, encouraging language throughout. You can also make a special place in your home where you can keep "the picture box." This place does not even need to be a box, it could be a drawer. At the end of the week, you will also have an opportunity to address all of the selected pictures rather than just the few you can with a group.

Exercise 8.
The Story Box

OBJECTIVE: To develop and enhance creative use of language. Expands both language comprehension and development.

WHEN TO DO: An integral part of any language arts curriculum. Great during circle or discussion time.

MATERIALS NEEDED: Decorated cartons, paper, marking pens, and a tape recorder.

DESCRIPTION: For groups: Most early childhood programs provide a time during the day when children are encouraged to volunteer information. Teachers should be prepared to regularly tape record these periods and transcribe individual children's stories at home. As in the "Picture Box" exercise, children should decorate their story boxes. Whenever they have a story to tell, they can talk to their teacher who will write it down and put it in one of the story boxes. All stories should have authors' names on them so children learn to personalize their stories.

At a designated time, a few stories should be selected and read aloud by the teacher. The author should be asked to make a dance to go with the story. The author can ask several children to accompany her or she can do a solo. Children can also be asked to respond to the story as a group. Again, this activity should be a mainstay in the language arts curriculum. As the year progresses, stories and dances will become more complex and detailed, as will the children's abilities.

For individuals: Since you are working with one child, you can usually transcribe a story spontaneously to be stored in a story box for later reflection, or you can respond to the story immediately.

◇ THE LANGUAGE DEVELOPMENT PROCESS: AGES SIX TO EIGHT ◇

The most important area of linguistic growth during the early school-age years is in language use. Throughout the school-age years, children increase their range of communication functions and learn how to become good conversational partners, how to make indirect requests, and how to process the language of the classroom. Two abilities enable young school-age children to become more effective communicators:

1. The ability to take the perspective of another person.
2. The ability to consider several aspects of a problem simultaneously.

For example, very young children can only see a conflict with a peer in terms of their own feelings and observations about what happened. Older children are able to negotiate, justify, and state reasons why they feel the way they do.

The ability to storytell also advances. Although children relate stories in the preschool years, by first grade, demands are placed on them to relate what truly can be considered a narrative, such as relating holiday experiences and vacation activities. These activities later appear in the form of written assignments. The ability to narrate or storytell is an important process in language development that involves a significant amount of creative thinking.

The older child also has the ability to maintain topics in conversation for long periods of time. Although younger children's ability to maintain conversation can be enhanced by adult intervention, the average three- or four-year-old can only exchange topics with a peer about 20 percent of the time. They are easily distracted and, as a result, their conversation can appear disjointed. The older child, however, can not only maintain topics but is also facile at introducing new ones.

The following Playdances stimulate the emerging discussion and conversation abilities so that school-age children can begin to use language as a means to problem solve and explore new experiences.

◊ LANGUAGE PLAYDANCES: AGES SIX TO EIGHT ◊

Exercise 1.
The Moving Picture

OBJECTIVE: To enhance creative use of language.

WHEN TO DO: During any art activity.

MATERIALS NEEDED: Pictures of fine art. Assorted art materials and music selections are optional.

DESCRIPTION: For groups and individuals: Children can relate to fine art at a surprisingly early age. In fact, it was Picasso himself who said we should not teach children to draw but learn from them instead. Children ages six to eight have a good feel for taking perspectives and should be encouraged to develop this skill. They can sense, for example, from looking at a painting or sculpture what a given artist may have been feeling or thinking about when she was working on the piece.

If it is convenient, take the children on a museum walk. Talk about the paintings they like and the ones they do not. If you can feed in some additional information about the lives of various artists, feel free to do so. Children can be surprisingly empathetic and insightful. When you have finished your walk, go to the museum bookstore and ask children to select a few postcards to bring home. (Note: The museum walk is not an absolute. If you have art books at home, it is perfectly acceptable to begin the activity there. However, if you can, the whole experience of the museum can make the activity all the more rich and exciting for children.)

At a subsequent time, sit down with the children and take a look at the postcards individually. Ask the children how a particular painting makes them feel and what it makes them think about. Give them a few minutes to construct a dance about this feeling or idea. They may want to add music or props. Again, give them time to flesh this experience out and complete it for themselves.

Children can construct their Playdances individually, in small clusters, or in one large group. In all cases, children should be given ample time to discuss their impressions of individual artworks (remember, this is a language enhancement activity), to add various pieces of music, and to construct both props and costumes.

Exercise 2.
Dancing Words

OBJECTIVE: To enhance creative use of language. A great comprehension exercise.

WHEN TO DO: As part of any language activity.

MATERIALS NEEDED: Brown craft paper, pencils or markers. Assorted art materials are optional.

DESCRIPTION: For groups and individuals: Tape several pieces of craft paper to the wall. Have the children generate as long a list of oppositional words as possible. For example: long/short, friendly/unfriendly, high/low, hard/soft, ugly/beautiful, or loud/quiet. Make the list as exhaustive as possible.

After the children are satisfied with their list, have them select three or four word pairs with which they would like to work. Be available to pose open-ended questions regarding the choices. For example, what do you think about when you think of beautiful? What would it be like to be very, very long?

If a child prefers, she can perform both word pair halves individually, constructing both a "loud" and a "quiet" dance. Or she can construct a word pair dance with a partner, each creating her or his own half. Parts can be alternated back and forth so that each child can have the opportunity to experience each word dance.

Remember, this is a language activity, so word choices do need to be discussed and illuminated in depth. For example, name all the things you can think of that are hot (small, sharp, perfect, sour, round, wet). Show me all the ways you can make your body sharp (square, black, tired, wonderful). Remember, some word pairs will be very concrete: high/low, big/small, while others will be extremely abstract: exciting/boring, dull/brilliant, horrible/wonderful, etc.

Exercise 3.
Haiku

OBJECTIVE: To enhance creative use of language. Effective as both a language comprehension and development activity.

WHEN TO DO: As part of any language expression activity.

MATERIALS NEEDED: Book of haiku.

DESCRIPTION: For groups: Begin to read aloud to the children from your haiku book.
Examples of haiku:

> *There a beggar goes!*
> *Heaven and earth he's wearing*
> *for his summer clothes.*

> *Well then, let us go*
> *to the place where we tumble*
> *down looking at snow.*

Have children stop you when they hear something interesting. Now read the interesting part again. Talk together about what the haiku means. Haiku is full of vital imagery and can be translated in many different ways. Often, the real meaning of the poem is hidden and needs to be explored with sensitive questioning. When everyone feels satisfied with the verbal exploration, ask the children to begin to construct their haiku Playdance.

As with all Playdances, they may want to embellish this activity by adding costumes, props, or music. Again, when constructing the Playdances, children can either perform solo, in pairs, or in large groups. The most important consideration is that children extend their haiku experiences to their own limits, using as many other art and music modalities as possible. Note: A variation of this activity is to have the children begin to write their own haiku and construct Playdances from these.

For individuals: With a single child, you might want to spend some extra time reading haiku aloud. Discussion here can also be extended and illuminated.

Exercise 4.
The Book Report

OBJECTIVE: To enhance creative use of language. A great activity for introducing the concept of plot or storyline, and characters.

WHEN TO DO: A mainstay in the language arts curriculum. A great prelude to beginning a writing workshop.

MATERIALS NEEDED: Any story and composition-style books.

DESCRIPTION: By the third or fourth grade, most children will be asked to write a book report. Many children have difficulty with this activity because they have never been asked to seriously consider how this report can or should be written. Writing a good report requires creative divergent thinking, not simply a rehashing of story events.

The creative thinking and sequencing skills required for a book report should begin early, in first and second grade. Here children can begin to build the foundation for concept development that will serve them for the rest of their academic lives.

Whenever children are read to, or read a story themselves, they should be encouraged to write about it in their reporting book. Reporting books can be their own, decorated to their heart's desire. Children should be provided with basic reporting information such as: characters are the people (animals, etc.) in the story; the plot or storyline is what happens to the characters.

Ideas are still very visual at this stage. So early stories will generally be a series of sequentially ordered pictures describing the plot as the child sees it. Children should add words to these pictures, depending upon their ability; however, spelling and grammar are not the priority now; ideas and their organization are.

Once children have created their picture-word stories, they should be asked to evaluate them in some way. Why did they like the story? Were there any parts they did not like? What were the parts or the characters they liked the best? Why?

Every stage of inquisition should cause reflection. Once a child is confident that her report is finished, she should be asked to dramatize the report using movement, music, props, or any combination thereof. The same time given for reflection on the report should be likewise generated for the dramatization.

By using movement and/or other modalities, an individual child can bring her classmates right into the action of the story. The physical experiencing of plot and characterization helps young children retain information and makes the entire process of reading all the more alluring.

For individuals: The personalization of the book report becomes far simpler with the individual child. Characters will, of course, have to be dramatized one at a time. What may be absent is the dynamics of an audience watching a final production. Particularly with an activity capitalizing upon characters and plot, audience reaction can be pivotal. When doing this activity at home, it may be wise to construct an audience of family and friends.

Exercise 5.
Something Special

OBJECTIVE: To enhance creative use of language.

WHEN TO DO: Another mainstay in the language arts curriculum.

An entire writing workshop curriculum can be built around this activity.

MATERIALS NEEDED: Composition-type books, pencils, and assorted art materials.

DESCRIPTION: For groups: Every child should have her own storytelling book, decorated individually. Every day, at a special time, children should be encouraged to write down their own special stories. These stories are different than those explored in the "Book Report" exercise. The "Book Report" stories are written by someone else. These are *their* stories. Invented spellings and awkward penmanship are the rule here. Grammatical corrections are saved for another time, and the free flow of spontaneous stories becomes the goal. First graders may initially have difficulty with this activity and can, of course, draw pictures to help them find their words. A few words, a few sentences, may be all that is available for the first few trials, and that is all that need be anticipated.

Once children are comfortable writing in their storytelling books, ask each child to select a story they really want to work on, one they like best. Tell them that all stories, like the books and nursery rhymes they have read, have a beginning, a middle, and an end. All stories have characters and something called a plot which is what happens to these characters during the story (see also Exercise 4, "The Book Report").

They need to think about how their story begins, what happens during their story, and what happens in the end. They need to think about who is in the story and why. All of these concepts need to be explored slowly and with care.

At each step of the story construction, children can be asked to use movement to clarify ideas, particularly if they are having difficulty. How would this character walk? How would they feel if they were hiding behind a door? Saw a crayon on the floor? Or made a sad, crying face?

Each child should create at her own pace. Some children may finish their stories more quickly than others, but this does not necessarily mean they are more facile. A thorough story exploration that takes time may prove the more distinguished.

As stories reach completion, children should be asked to dramatize their story with dance, music, costumes, and words. They can perform their stories alone, with a partner, or in a small group. These dramatizations need not be elaborate, but children should take time to organize and communicate ideas. Remember, at this stage of development, children are honing their abilities to monitor and evaluate their work independently. Before they present a story, they should feel confident about the final product.

For individuals: When giving attention to just one child, the development of stories may take less time but should not be less thoughtful. Also, in this instance, children will need to think about just one character, or a series of characters they can perform alone. You are always available as an addition but for the most part, this storytelling will be a solitary adventure versus a collective one.

Exercise 6.
The Movie Review

OBJECTIVE: To enhance the creative use of language.

WHEN TO DO: As part of the language arts curriculum. A good focus for discussion group.

MATERIALS NEEDED: A tape recorder.

DESCRIPTION: For groups or individuals: Children often have the opportunity to go to the movies or watch videos at home, yet this activity is essentially passive. Children are rarely asked to reflect intelligently upon what they have seen.

During a group discussion time, ask children to think about a movie they have seen. It could be one they have seen recently or one seen long ago. One at a time, children should be asked to speak into the tape recorder describing a particular aspect of the movie: a character, an interesting story line, an actor or actress, etc. and why they liked or did not like it. In the course of discussing the film, they should compare and contrast it to other films they have seen, like a movie review.

Before they move on to the next step, children should be allowed to practice their reviews on the tape recorder until they are satisfied with the result. Once they are satisfied, they will need to dramatize either the entire review or a portion of it. After listening to another's review, they may also decide that they want to work on this one, rather than their own. Whatever they choose, their Playdance should directly reflect the content of the review. For example, an interpretation of a specific character, the sequence of events in the plot, the climax or other emotionally dynamic point in the film should be discussed. Children can use the recording of the review as a backdrop for their action, or they can select an alternative such as a piece of music or even silence.

Exercise 7.
Vacation Spots

OBJECTIVE: To enhance creative use of language.

WHEN TO DO: Particularly effective after a vacation break.

MATERIALS NEEDED: Cartons, assorted art materials, and props.

DESCRIPTION: For groups or individuals: Children should decorate a number of cartons as if they were luggage. The idea is for children to choose a vacation spot, either real or imagined, and then pack for that particular excursion: the beach, Disney World, Grandma's, or even outer space! They can create the items packed from classroom materials, bring in the real thing, or use various props as symbols, for example, a small broom for a boating oar, a blanket for an evening gown, etc. Once children have assembled these materials, they should be asked to dramatize the vacation's events, using the items they have packed away.

Language comprehension, processing, and expression skills can significantly impact a child's thinking, problem-solving abilities, social interactions, attention, and memory. The proficiency with which young children use language in their daily lives influences what they can attend to, how they connect new experiences to what they already understand, and what information they can apply appropriately. Teachers and parents need to remove the abstractness of language and replace it with what the young child already knows and understands: her moving body.

Yet the processes of self-awareness and language acquisition are not solely responsible for the emergence of the creative child. Much current research indicates that how and what children can learn from their peers is very different from what they learn from adults. Not less important, just different. True creativity involves interaction, consolidation, and collaboration. Read on!

◇ *CHAPTER 8* ◇

Interpersonal Skills: Getting to Know You

Dancing is the most individual of all movements, but even dancing would be pointless without an audience; in other words, without some social or transcendental aim

MARIA MONTESSORI, THE ABSORBENT MIND

Alex: Tony, I didn't see you for a long time.
Tony: I was at my grandma's.
Alex: Someone told me you were at your grandma's.
Tony: Did you want me?
Alex: Yes, I wanted you lots of times.

Someone once said that there were only two or three human stories, yet they went on fiercely repeating themselves as if they had never happened before. Perhaps the most significant of these stories is discovering other human beings and reaching out and expressing our feelings to them—like three-and-a-half-year-olds Alex and Tony above.

Yet the reason these stories hold such magnetism for us is not the nature of the stories themselves, but the fact that the characters continually change. Each new character gives vitality to the same old story. For as long as I have been teaching, observing, and parenting, I have been drawn to try to understand not only the similarities of

---

"storyline" in young children's social development, but also the uniqueness of each child as well. How could one explain the wonderfully unique variations on the general theme of early social development?

I suspect that, initially, many parents, including myself, have the rather naive view that social development is a kind of popularity contest. Social ability is measured by counting how many friends you have or how many party invitations you receive. And surely both popular and unpopular children exist, but most children would be better off described in terms of the kind of social person they are and the kinds of social relationships they are likely to have. Just as each of us has our own unique personality, each of us has a unique constellation of social abilities that provide us with the tools to form satisfying social relationships. Not everyone can be a leader or a social butterfly, nor should everyone try to be.

I began to look for answers. I looked at my own children. I looked at my friends' children. I observed children in funded daycare, in posh, urban private schools, and in middle-class suburban classrooms. I saw bright, gifted children and severely handicapped ones. And in each case, the same reality rang true. Popular children were not all alike, nor were unpopular children. In fact, it was the exceptions that proved the rule.

I remember one glaring example one afternoon seated in my friend, Janet's, living room. There was a huge clamor in her playroom, and I ran back to see who or what was causing such a commotion. Evidently, there were two children vying for a third's attention. The two attention viers were engaged in a series of gymnastic feats on a small portable trampoline. Two girls were trying to outdo each other to impress the third child, a boy. Daniel was seated on the playroom floor, dressed in an elaborate cowboy outfit, shouting praises, and urging on the girls. He was one of the most charismatic and creative individuals I had ever seen.

I left the playroom and sat for some time with Daniel's mother and Janet, commenting on David's amazing social ability. Janet confirmed my opinion, stating that if there were a Prince Charming, Daniel most certainly fit the bill. It was only when Daniel and his mother prepared to leave that I noticed not only was Daniel not particularly good looking, but he was mildly handicapped as well. I knew then that all children had the ability to have meaningful social relationships, no matter how different they were. In fact, it was the nurturing of these individual differences and the focus upon creativity that could make all the difference.

That is why it is so important for teachers and parents to be able to identify each child's individual creative style and to develop strategies to help children use their particular styles to their advantage. One of the most important jobs we have as adults is to help children discover who they are, how to like themselves, and how to share who they are with others.

◇ *HOW DO CHILDREN LEARN TO MAKE FRIENDS?* ◇

There is much for adults to learn when it comes to helping children discover the pleasures of friendship.

Mimi and *Sherry*

> *Mimi:* You're a poo-poo, dooey head! Oh! Oh! Oh!
>   [laughing]
> *Sherry:* Stinko! Ayuk, ayuk! Yeah!
> *Mimi:* I'm funny? Right? I'm really funny!
> *Sherry:* Yeah, yeah—you stinko adooey-head!

Lisa and *Auguste*

> *Lisa:* I have a new dress. It's pink.
> *Auguste:* Oh, I like pink. I do. It's my favorite, favorite color.
> *Lisa:* Do you like it? Do you, do you?
> *Auguste:* Oh, yes. It's stunning, stunning! I love pink and other
>   colors too . . .

Mimi and Sherry interact comically; Lisa and Auguste are more contained, even charming. As different as children are socially, most are able to make good friends with the support of teachers and parents, and these friendship-making skills are ones they will use the rest of their lives.

Children learn much about relationships by watching and listening to other children and by how others react to them. Some children show others how they feel readily and fearlessly. Others need a great deal of support when they deal with another child. Yet all children need to figure out how to behave until they have a friend. When someone approaches, they need to work out how to get that person's attention. If there has been a fight or a struggle, they have to find out how to win back the hurt or angry friend. Parents often fail to realize just how much problem-solving is involved in making and holding onto friendships. Making friends involves much more than similar interests or good feelings. Everyday, young children are actively building working models of their social world. Everyday, they are building a picture of themselves, what makes other people tick, and what causes a relationship to run smoothly or turn sour.

Social skills, like everything else in life, are primarily acquired through learning: observation, modeling, and rehearsal. And although humans are theorized to be preset from birth with a set of behaviors that elicit social responsiveness, these behaviors need to be nurtured. They will not develop in a vacuum.

◇ WHY IS MAKING FRIENDS SO IMPORTANT? ◇

Making friends is *The* central human experience for adults and children alike. No one needs to tell us this. We simply know it to be true. How often do we hear people talking about how friendly, or unfriendly, they are with one person or another? Not only is friend-making central to our experience as humans, but it is also vital to our growth and well-being. Statistically, people with strong friendships live longer, enjoy better health, and are just plain happier than those without close friends. In a world as socially demanding as ours, the single most common reason parents give for enrolling their child in nursery school is so she can make friends. No one wants to be *All Alone.* In fact, being all alone all the time is perhaps the most frightening nightmare of all, particularly for young children.

Piaget, the famed Swiss psychologist who explored the development of intelligence in young children, believed that every child is born with a vast, unspecifiable, and indeterminable social potential: the ability to touch others. Yet this power to make friends, to reach out to another human being and express our feelings to them, is not the same for everyone. Mimi and Sherry, Lisa and Auguste, Alex and Tony, all touched each other, but they all did it in distinctly different ways. Mimi used humor; Auguste, flattery; Tony empathy. Any group of young children, or adults for that matter, is always composed of a wide variety of social types or styles. Some are flamboyant and excitable, others are quieter and intuitive. This is not to say that children do not have many sides to their individual personalities. They do. The most gentle of children has a tough, swaggering side; the most assertive, a warm, endearing one. Yet most of us could pretty much characterize ourselves as displaying certain social features more than we do others. It is important that we are all different. It does, as the adage says, take all social types to make a world.

Unfortunately, our society has traditionally rewarded certain social types more than others, particularly in the classroom. Fun-loving, out-going types, like Mimi and Sherry, get lots of attention; while the more sensitive types , like Tony and Alex, slip through the cracks. As we move down the developmental scale and into daycare, these social differences become strikingly apparent. Three-year-olds do not know the rules of the game yet. Wait your turn, don't push, and be charming to get what you want have not registered. All these children have are their basic social instincts. But the fact that they are young does not always stop adults or other children from making rash, and often unfair, judgments.

The teacher's and parents' contact with the child help her determine her self-worth before she has other meaningful ties. If the teacher has

If the teacher has an accepting, interested, and appreciative attitude, the child has a good chance of developing one.

an accepting, interested, and appreciative attitude, the child has a good chance of developing one. In fact, this nonjudgmental, accepting attitude is also the stamp of all good friendships, and is the foundation of nurturing creativity in the classroom.

Yet children often behave in ways that puzzle and concern the most experienced or patient teacher. We must first distinguish between "bad" behavior and behavior that is only tiresome or inconvenient to adults. Researchers have been particularly unkind when typing social characteristics in children. Chess and Thomas's temperament scale includes: 1. the easy child; 2. the difficult child; and 3. the slow to warm-up child.[1]

Batcher's social types in the classroom include: the battered child, the teacher's pet, the good student, the thorn, the bad kid, the charmer, the tyrant, or the prima donna.[2]

Now honestly, outside of the "easy" child and the "good" student, would you want your own child known to the world as being a member of any of the other categories? I wouldn't. And what makes a child "bad" or "difficult"? Was it the child, or the way people reacted to her? Surely, I am committed to the idea that all children are not wonderful all the time. But a difficult child was usually difficult because that was the message she was given. How can you foster self-esteem when you have just labeled someone a thorn? Repeated conferences with parents and teachers have told me that these labels are not only damaging to the children who have to live with them, but also to the adults who begin to see their dinner tables and classrooms filled with tyrants and prima donnas, rather than eager, loving children.

Years of research have taught me many things about human development. First of all, most kids are potential easy children and good students. It is the manner in which they are perceived and accepted that is important. The most different of children can be helped to feel surprisingly good about herself, and anyone who likes herself has a far easier time socially than someone who does not. Secondly, neither easy children nor good students are all alike. Children differ a great deal more in form than they do in degree. It is the way children do things that is significant, not how much or how little of it they do. The child with one good friend can be just as happy

[1]Chess, Stella and Thomas, Alexander. *Temperament in Clinical Practice*. Los Angeles, CA: Western Psychological Services, 1989.
[2]Batcher, Elaine. *Emotion in the Classroom*. New York: Praeger Press, 1981.

and well adjusted as the child with three friends, perhaps even more so.

Yet young children's social abilities are often difficult to discern because they have so often been underutilized or misdirected. A child's unique constellation of social abilities is as individual and clear as a set of fingerprints. Once you recognize them, you can begin to provide her with a specialized set of experiences that will instill self-esteem and self-confidence.

As one teacher confided in me: "I feel so much better now that I understand Lisa, and so does Lisa. I was always pushing her to play with other kids. Not that she didn't play at all, but I just couldn't understand her need to be by herself so much. You see, I'm not like that. When Lisa wants to play with a friend, she does, and when she wants to be alone, she does. I need to be with people almost all the time. Lisa's different, not less competent, just different."

Children generally seek approval by doing the things we ask them to. Many young children behave this way, but evidence shows that it is *belonging*, not necessarily approval, that is important for most children. If approval were the most important object, children would simply make themselves into whatever another wanted. Children may take any one of many avenues in their search for acceptance. It is interesting that many children seem to know who belongs but are less certain of how they can belong.

The previous chapters dealt with aspects of self-awareness and language that would lead young children toward the ultimate collaborative skills involved in creativity. Yet the aspect of belonging is perhaps the most significant element to address when attempting to have children function as a group. To belong, children need the following skills:

Self-Control

- compromising
- responding to teasing
- accepting/giving criticism
- responding to pushing
- questioning unfair rules

Communication with Peers

- asking to join
- greeting people

- introducing yourself
- inviting others to join
- asking for help
- offering help
- refusing unreasonable requests

Classroom Cooperation

- following rules
- taking turns
- listening to instructions
- ignoring distractions
- waiting for help

These are all important social abilities for young children to learn during early childhood. Yet these ends are best achieved when children really do believe they are part of a group in which *they do belong*. This feeling of belonging is generated when children's individual creative instincts are nurtured. No child should feel "weird." Teachers should take measures to prevent children from being scapegoated, and should prevent themselves from becoming too friendly with a particularly endearing child.

Research has demonstrated that children with limited opportunity for social interaction often behave quite differently from those with rich peer involvements. Providing creative opportunities for social interaction and play is a central objective of early childhood education.

Mastering social and emotional skills is clearly one of the objectives of the young child's basic activities. Play and other nonverbal behaviors have been widely acknowledged as an instrumental factor in social learning. Through movement activities, children may observe others, invent and test out new ideas, and acquire new interpersonal skills and competencies. Social events, unlike purely physical experiences, do not of themselves have order and meaning, but are the construction of human beings. Social events do not in themselves make sense. It is we who make them meaningful through our understanding. We do this by a process of self-indication, essentially an inner dialogue, whereby we come to terms with what is happening around us and make it meaningful to us. A child's acceptance by her peers is a potent factor in her well-being. In addition, what one learns from one's peers is essentially different from what one learns from her

Play and other nonverbal behaviors have been widely acknowledged as instrumental factors in social learning.

parents or other family members. Although opinion remains divided about how children become socialized, it appears that children learn to become like other people in their culture as a result of identifying with its members and by being encouraged to display desirable social behaviors.

The Playdances in this chapter reinforce creative collaborative effort while simultaneously developing necessary social abilities. A few suggestions for nurturing interpersonal skills in all age groups follow:

Continue to help children build a positive self-image. Being able to reach out to others begins with a healthy self-concept; so adults must do all they can to help children like themselves and to feel good about trying to do things.

Allow children to help you in the classroom. What a big help you are! Thanks for putting away the markers!

Help children feel good about their bodies. Look at these pictures!

Remember how little you used to be? Can you name some things you can do now, you couldn't do then?

Allow children to make their own choices. Well, it's another cold day. See those clothes over there? Why don't you pick out what you think you should wear?

Listen to children and acknowledge their feelings. Gee, that sounds awful. That must have made you upset.

Provide a friendly model. You know, today Mrs. Graham's not feeling well. Let's go to her class and cheer her up.

Provide many opportunities for children to interact with other children. Seat children in pairs as often as you can. The dyad, or pair, is our primary unit of communication and collaboration.

Allow children to choose their own friends. Respect their choices, even if you do not understand them. The most important factor is that these relationships are nurturant to children.

Respect individual children's social style. This is a most important lesson to be learned. Some children need many friends, others just a few.

◊ THE DEVELOPMENT OF INTERPERSONAL SKILLS: AGES THREE TO FIVE ◊

Children's conceptions of collaborative effort develop from a primitive association of the sharing of material goods or physical experiences, like rolling or hanging off the swing bars, to a more advanced understanding of the sharing of private thoughts and feelings. Younger children establish and maintain contact by sharing and playing with one another, whereas older children are more likely to offer others assistance and, ultimately, acceptance. Quantitative models of development do not have much to offer in the study of children's social knowledge. For example, children demonstrate very early some knowledge of reciprocity (I give, you give), but it is the form rather than the amount that changes with development.

The Playdances for three- to five-year-olds work to form relationships in one-to-one activities, which foster concepts of belonging and acceptance. Here creative efforts are established through the sharing and knowledge of specific materials and activities.

Exercise 1.
Tied Together

OBJECTIVE: To enhance the concept of sharing in interaction.

WHEN TO DO: A great entry activity for any social skill curriculum.

MATERIALS NEEDED: Large elastic bands, enough for two children to stretch at least three feet away from one another.

DESCRIPTION: For groups: Have children separate into pairs with partners of their own selection. They can sit, stand, start on all fours, or any combination thereof including one up, one down. Slide the elastic bands over their waists, and put on some music; almost any bright rhythm will do. The idea is for children to begin to experiment pushing and pulling, first one child taking the lead, then the other. The elastic band causes the receiving child to respond almost immediately to the physical movements and demands of the leading child. In this way, children receive very physical information about the roles of assertion, submission, and reciprocation. As always, children should be queried about their own social preferences: Did they like being a leader? Was there anything they didn't like about it? Did they enjoy being a follower?

Additionally, several children can be placed inside a single band, one leading, then two, with all of the others following. Although children will not be able to fully integrate some of the concepts presented here, such as the differences, strengths, and difficulties presented by having one as opposed to two leaders, children can be probed after the activity with questions such as: What felt better, one leader or two? Why do you think so? Were things easier with one or many followers, etc.?

For individuals: With very little modification, this activity can be easily conducted at home. Of course, you may have to recruit additional family members for the latter portion of the exercise.

Exercise 2.
Touching Others

Teachers should be sensitive about "touching activities" in the early childhood curriculum. There is concern related to very real issues of child abuse and neglect. Careless use of these activities could result in misinterpretation. However, appropriate use can enhance the child's understanding of appropriate versus inappropriate touching by adults and/or other children.

OBJECTIVE:	To begin to develop the concept of sharing feelings.
WHEN TO DO:	Early in any social skill curriculum. A focusing activity.
DESCRIPTION:	For groups or individuals: Have children sit in pairs with partners of their own selection. Tell the children that you want them to listen to each other's bodies. One can begin by putting his ear to the other child's back or tummy and really listening to what is going on. The insides of our bodies are chock-full of wonderful sounds. After they have finished listening, demonstrate a simple neck, shoulder, or back massage. Some children may be ticklish, but most accept this physical contact willingly after a few seconds.
	The idea is to get children to really sense what their partner is feeling and to respond to those needs. Some children will want a gentle massage, others a more vigorous one. Some will want their hands rubbed. All children should be given an opportunity to explore how to give the massage, and, equally important, how to receive one.

Exercise 3.
Finger Friends

OBJECTIVE:	To foster concept of interaction.
WHEN TO DO:	A great language arts as well as social skill activity; also great as dramatic play.
MATERIALS NEEDED:	Assorted craft and arts materials.

Exercise:
Touching Others

DESCRIPTION: For groups or individuals: Tell the children they are
going to make some "finger friends." Assemble a
variety of construction materials. Finger puppets can
be made a hundred different ways, and children
should be encouraged to explore alternatives.

The construction of finger friends may take several
sessions, so be patient. Children can make finger
friends for one finger or all five. Older four- and
five-year-olds may be able to construct several
characters from a familiar story. Younger children
will be more able to make family or community
members: doctor, fireman, etc. Remember, young
children are still honing hand skills and struggling
with symbols at this stage, so their constructions are
expected to be rough around the edges.

Once children have at least two finger friends
completed, the friends can begin talking to each
other. One child can begin by creating the voice for
both friends. When children have had individual
experiences talking for both of their puppets,
children can be asked to select partners so that
different sets of finger friends can begin talking. Once
children have had their puppets talk, it is time to get
them moving. How would one finger friend move as
opposed to another? How would they move
together? Children should be encouraged to make

many finger friend dances, exploring as many interactional styles as possible.

◇ THE DEVELOPMENT OF INTERPERSONAL SKILLS: AGES SIX TO EIGHT ◇

During this later stage of early childhood, there is the obvious movement in children's interpersonal knowledge from an understanding of the material basis for contact to an understanding of the psychological basis. As stated earlier, friendship for three- to five-year-olds is clearly associated with playing and sharing toys. When playing is initiated, liking and friendship almost automatically follow. Beginning in kindergarten, children also start to assist each other when they sense another could use this assistance.

By the time the child enters first grade, two new levels of interpersonal skills emerge:

1. The concept that friendship or collaboration exists as the reciprocal interest of two parties, and that each party must respond to the other's needs or desires.
2. The concept that friends are people who understand one another, and share their inner thoughts with one another, their feelings and secrets. Friends are in a special position to help each other with special and/or difficult feelings.

Much of this work in perspective taking, collaborative effort, and sharing of special feelings or ideas, can be accomplished through the use of group Playdances that focus upon the development of these specific skills.

◇ INTERPERSONAL SKILL PLAYDANCES: AGES SIX TO EIGHT ◇

Exercise 1.
What Do You See?

OBJECTIVE: To foster the concept of shared thought or feeling.

WHEN TO DO: As part of any social skills curriculum.

MATERIALS NEEDED:	Large sheets of craft paper, finger paint, watercolor, and masking tape.
DESCRIPTION:	For groups: You can start this activity in pairs or small groups. Give each cluster a large sheet of paper and help them tape it to the floor. Each group can select their own paints. The idea is for each child to have a turn pouring or splattering some paint across the paper into some indiscriminate shapes. Children should have time to consider how different colors and shapes interact with one another to form a single distinct pattern. Ask questions such as: Is that the design you expected? Why do you think the color changed so? These questions should be posed to encourage reflection on the process. Once individual groups of children are satisfied with the design they have splashed, a volunteer group can be asked for an improvised Playdance to reflect their creation.

These improvised Playdances will be slightly different than those they have considered before. Here the children should be conscious of creating the dance together-as-one. Their dance should no longer merely be a sum of its parts, as perhaps earlier Playdances had been, but instead a unified whole. As the splash painting reflects a new result from different tangles of color and shape, so should the movements of the Playdance. These are not a group of soloists performing, but a duet, a trio, or a quartet all striving for perfect harmony with each other.

For individuals: The format or focus of this Playdance is *not* applicable for the one-to-one setting.

Exercise 2.
Body Sculpture

OBJECTIVE:	To encourage cooperative effort and to introduce the concept of passive versus active interaction.
WHEN TO DO:	A good activity before or after a museum visit.
DESCRIPTION:	For groups: Before you begin this exercise, gather some pictures of sculpture and have your class discuss them together. Explain that some sculptures are representations: models of real things. Others are

Exercise:
Body Sculpture

abstract: designs that artists invent in their heads. Children can also experiment with clay and other sculpting materials before progressing to the movement activity.

Once children have discussed their impressions of various sculpture, have one child lie down on the floor for your demonstration. Begin to pat her or roll her as you would a piece of clay. Have the other children select partners and begin to do the same, one child being the sculptor, the other the clay. Children acting as the sculptors should be able to mold their "clay" into a desired shape, the "clay" remaining passive yet somewhat responsive. Children should exchange roles, each child having a turn as both the sculptor and the clay.

When children are comfortable with this exchange, one sculptor should be assigned a group of children as her clay. Instead of having a single piece, she will have many. The sculptor will now have to consider many shapes, sizes, and body types as she orchestrates her body sculpture. She can experiment using her clay bodies in many different ways. As always, any Playdance should include reflection: Why did you think that sculpture worked while the other one didn't? What was the feeling you were trying to say with this sculpture?

For individuals: The first portion of "Body Sculpture" is adaptable to the individual child. The second, collective portion, requires other members.

Exercise 3.
Be Someone Else

OBJECTIVE: To enhance perspective-taking and the emergence of empathy.

WHEN TO DO: A great language activity when you are beginning your discussion of character.

MATERIALS NEEDED: Cartoon videotapes.

DESCRIPTION: For groups: Although any videotapes of people can be useful in this activity, young children most readily respond to concrete images. Cartoon characters are purposefully caricatured so that children can immediately discern general personality features.

Have children assemble to watch a few video clips. Emphasize that they are not watching these videos for the sake of enjoying the individual episodes, but to observe the individual characters very carefully. How do they move? What is it about their movements that tells us something about them?

Each child should select a character to portray from one of the videotapes. Keeping their chosen character a secret from the others, children should develop the movements of their individual character so she is easily recognizable. Each character should be presented one at a time in a kind of guessing-game format.

Teachers should be ready with probing questions whether or not the children are able to guess which character is being portrayed: How did you know that was . . . ? What did she do with her body that told you this . . . ? What are other movements that could help us identify this character?

For individuals: This Playdance is readily adaptable to individual children in its present format. The guessing game would, of course, be a simple platform of two, but the questions posed should be no less probing. As members of the same family, you and your child might choose to portray some family member or close friend, using a home video as a starting point.

Exercise 4.
Masks

OBJECTIVE: To enhance perspective-taking ability and the development of empathy.

WHEN TO DO: A wonderful Halloween activity, although equally effective when exploring the practices of different cultures.

MATERIALS NEEDED: Assorted ethnic or Halloween-type masks.

DESCRIPTION: For groups or individuals: About the best time to buy masks during the year is right before Halloween. Even the simple Five-and-Dime variety is quite extensive. For about $2 a piece you can easily develop a healthy collection. If you are fortunate enough to have acquired some ethnic masks on your travels, all the better.

Simply spread all the masks out on a carpet for the children to inspect. Give them time to select a mask from which they will create a Playdance and time to really look at it. Remember what they choose to attribute to the mask will actually be part of themselves. If you have some mirrors in the room, have the children look at themselves with their masks. Allow them to improvise and work out some movement patterns for their mask. They can add some music, if they choose, but many of these mask dances are actually most dramatic when performed in silence or with only a single drum beat.

Each child should be given a turn to perform her mask dance. They can perform in solo, but some children may want to work something out with a partner or a small cluster of three. As always, children should be encouraged to reflect on their Playdance describing why they chose the mask and the movements.

Exercise 5.
Walk Like the Animal

OBJECTIVE: To enhance perspective-taking.

WHEN TO DO: A great science or nature activity. Also a good accompaniment to a zoo visit.

MATERIALS NEEDED: Pictures and/or videos of various animals.

DESCRIPTION: For groups or individuals: This is the time to gather all those *National Geographics* you have been harboring and bring them to class. You can ask the children to do likewise as many of them will have similar contributions from home. You can compile pictures of interesting animals in a variety of ways. Children can make their own animal books or you can drape poster collages across the walls. It would also be beneficial to rent or borrow some *National Geographic* films. Many of these are readily available at your local video store. Seeing how various animals move gives them an added dimension.

Once children have visually explored a number of animals, have each select two or three that they would like to portray. Children can present dramatizations by themselves, in pairs, or in small groups. Encourage the selection of animals with opposing characteristics: a tiger and a chimp, for example. Children identify and personalize differences more readily than similarities.

Once children have honed these portrayals and presented them to the group, you can ask them if any one of these animals remind them of people they know. We often refer to people by using animal names. We might say someone is a "bull," a "tiger," a "pussy cat," a "crab," a "pig," a "peacock," a

"lamb," etc. Can they think of other names?
Why do they think we use these names?

Have each child choose an animal name and see if she could move like that kind of person. How would a snake move as opposed to a horse? How about if the snake-person and the horse-person were having lunch together, or walking down the street? How might they act together? The combinations here are endless, and can provide a great deal of insight for young children.

Exercise 6.
Opposites

OBJECTIVE: To enhance the concept of shared feeling and empathy.

WHEN TO DO: An excellent language arts activity as well as a social skill activity.

DESCRIPTION: For groups: Have the children compile lists of opposite words: round/straight, cold/hot, stinky/fragrant, stop/go, smooth/scratchy, in/out, huge/tiny, brave/frightened, shiny/dull.

Again, the list is not exhaustive. Write down the opposite pairs and place them in a covered shoebox (this is just one variation; you can collect your list of opposites in many other acceptable ways.)

Have children select partners. Ask children to try to find someone they do not ordinarily Playdance with. This may meet with some resistance, but do try. Each pair reaches into the box and selects an opposite. Quietly, they plot how the opposites can be dramatized. The idea is for each member of the duet to alternate between parts. As this is an improvisation and they do not know their partners well, they will need to inspect their movements very carefully. For example, if they are portraying "hot and cold," as one moves from hot to cold, the other moves from cold to hot. The changes should be gradual, each complementing the movements of the other. When a pair is finished with their opposite dance, they should be asked to consider what clues each gave to the other that change was about to occur.

For individuals: This Playdance is not applicable for a one-to-one situation.

Programs that use peer interaction to foster self-esteem and self-actualization stimulate children's creative potentials by providing a wide range of experiences. Children are expected to take larger roles in their own creative development through their choice of partners, activities, and their own active interest in the world.

In our mechanized society, the awareness of I and you appears to be fading. Children can regain this awareness by dancing together. Every child dances in a special way because every human creature moves in her own rhythms. Dance sharpens the perceptions of human uniqueness.

◊ *CHAPTER 9* ◊

The Talented Child: Identifying Giftedness

Everyone is born with genius, but most people only keep it a few minutes

MARTHA GRAHAM, NEW YORK TIMES INTERVIEW, MARCH 31, 1985

Most of our schools place a real penalty upon being different. Yet as I have staunchly reiterated throughout *Playdancing*, all creativity is dependent upon just that: being different. All children, given the right avenues for creative expression, can achieve remarkable things. However, every once in a while, teachers and parents are faced with the truly exceptional child. She is not necessarily the child with the highest IQ, the best test scores, or the most precious verbal ability. In fact, adults through no fault of their own, can be downright amiss in identifying truly talented children.

> *The grown-up's response was to advise me to set aside my drawings . . . and devote myself instead to geography, history, arithmetic, and grammar. That is why, at the age of six, I gave up what might have a magnificent career as a painter. . . . Grown-ups never understand anything by themselves, and it is tiresome for children to be always and forever explaining things to them.*[1]

---

[1]De Saint-Exupéry, Antoine. *The Little Prince.* New York: Harcourt, Brace, & World, 1943.

It's been a good fifty years since De Saint-Exupéry penned *The Little Prince*, yet creativity is still undervalued. Not that adults are uninterested in exceptional ability; they are more interested in exceptional ability than ever before, and toys and materials that promise success for young children are produced at an all-time high. The problem is that most teachers and parents simply cannot identify a talented child. Few researchers have devoted attention to studying talented children who have superior ability in the creative arts. Talent, as a term, has been used instead to mean gifted, creative, or academically superior in other-than artistic pursuits.

The attitude of the grown-ups in *The Little Prince*, who advised the child to discard his drawings and devote himself to more important subjects, belittle the child's superior artistic ability. Many children have had adults react in a similar fashion to their emerging artistic talent. It was only as recently as 1972 that artistically talented students were acknowledged by the federal government as a population worthy of attention. Sydney Marland, issuer of the *Marland Report*, provided legislation and thus a major opportunity to implement research and develop programs to meet the needs of exceptionally talented children. However, neither the *Marland Report* nor any subsequent legislation provides an operational definition of what it is to be artistically talented.[2] Yet we do know that these abilities appear strikingly early in development and thus are essential for early childhood teachers to recognize and nurture. Rather than continuing to harp upon what we do not know, let's examine what we do.

First of all, talented children are not necessarily well-liked or appreciated by adults or other children. This is not necessarily their fault. Remember our society rewards conformity. These children may not be well-rounded, will often attempt difficult or even dangerous tasks, and constantly struggle with sanctions against diversity. This may make them appear belligerent or confrontational. They often find that maintaining their level of creativity alienates potential friendships and thus many suffer from psychological estrangement—not unlike some of their exceptional adult counterparts.

On the upside, they do have a high level of effective intelligence and an openness to experience. They are not preoccupied with the impressions of others, are independent, and have a genuine candor about their abilities. They are interested in meanings and implications,

[2]Marland, Sydney. (1972) Education of the Gifted and Talented, volume 2. Background papers submitted to the U.S. Office of Education. Washington D.C.: U.S. Government Printing Office.

not minute details or facts as such, and delight in the unfinished and the challenging.

Secondly, and I feel this point is particularly enlightening, almost all talented children have had significantly unhappy childhood experiences. Does this mean we need to contribute to this pool of unhappy experiences? Absolutely not. But we do need to think what exactly does a state of unhappiness cause one to do? Most often, turn inward and reflect. It is a sad comment on our society that one of the only opportunities we have to turn inward and reflect is when we are depressed or deprived. As teachers, we need to begin to implement other opportunities like those outlined in *Playdancing*.

Lastly, social pressure is perhaps the most powerful quencher of talent in young children. In their early efforts to be liked, some talented children may choose to hide or downplay their real abilities. Parents may fear their child's eventual alienation and encourage her to be modest, and not to be a show-off. It takes a courageous soul to pursue ability with such limited moral support. This may be why only the independently talented ever succeed. The more dependently talented may never have the opportunity.

Which brings me to an interesting question. Is it that talented children are really unhappy, confrontational loners or does our society make them that way? Are these more or less negatively viewed qualities ones that artists must develop to elbow their way through a society essentially unsupportive of artistic endeavor. I do not have a final answer to this question but it is one that both teachers and parents of young children need to consider. Identification is key. In the right environment, the talented child's uniqueness can be appreciated and enhanced, regardless of her personality.

◇ *THINGS TO LOOK FOR* ◇

The following are attributes recognized as those possessed by many talented children. The list is not exhaustive. Some children may possess a large percentage of these characteristics, others just a few.

- verbal behavior is characterized by a richness of expression, elaboration, and fluency
- has storehouse of information on a variety of topics unusual for her age
- has good retention of information

- becomes easily absorbed in tasks, may be difficult for her to transition
- is easily bored with routine
- needs little, if any, external motivation to follow through in a self-selected activity
- displays a great deal of curiosity, constantly asking questions
- generates unusual solutions to problems
- confidently expresses radical opinions
- is tenacious
- incorporates a wide variety of materials into artwork, continually varies subject and content
- seeks out opportunities to hear and create music
- perceives fine differences in musical tone such as pitch and loudness
- easily remembers melodies and can reproduce them accurately
- is an interesting storyteller
- conveys information nonverbally through gestures, facial expressions, and body language
- easily determines what resources are necessary for accomplishing a task
- grasps the relationship of individual steps to a whole process

All of the aforementioned characteristics are explored with some depth in the Playdancing program. As each child is encouraged to achieve her potential, it matters not what this potential is. Playdancing is not a contest.

With the Playdancing program, the talented child need not be pulled out for enrichment as they are in some public schools. The enrichment is right in the classroom for everyone to experience. Why should only the gifted or talented have enrichment? The concepts of "mainstreaming," "individualized educational programming," and "acceleration" are best met with a curriculum that encourages abilities and ideas. Any program for young talented children must recognize the relationship of that program to the basic research and factors affecting the growth and development of all young children. Playdancing was developed to directly address the uniqueness and gifts of each and every child. Even so, more research needs to be conducted and more information collected concerning the needs of talented children.

◇ *AFTERWORD* ◇

The battle over the true meaning of education is continually waged. Do we teach children what we already know or teach them to ask new questions? The reality is that children do need a basic knowledge about themselves and their world to ask the questions that need to be asked. But this need for basic information should not be a substitute for independent thinking.

Creative expression has never been primary in our culture. Many say that it is our pioneer spirit and concern with the practical that has led us down the path of logic, creating our great, though perhaps uninspired, history. Yet the most primitive and survival-oriented cultures on earth have made art, music, and movement central to their community lives.

The absence of ritual in our culture is being felt. We rarely mark the passing of time in more than cursory ways. Family, religion, government, and education—all those institutions that we have traditionally looked toward for guidance—are fumbling for new direction. We cannot look to old simple remedies to solve our new complex problems. We need thinkers, doers, and idea-makers!

We must keep a place for art and creative expression in our schools, regardless of the trend for basic skills. To do that, teachers and parents need to be politically active. Write to your congressmen and congresswomen. Find out who is on your State Education Committee. Get a copy of the Federal Register. Find out what is being funded and why. Get involved in your community board. Do not let others make decisions for your children without them knowing your views. We all have rights and we all have responsibility. Remember, science may help explain life, but art and creative expression is what we live for. Let us help our children live their lives to the fullest potential possible.

◊ SELECTED BIBLIOGRAPHY ◊

Amabile, Teresa M. *The Social Psychology of Creativity*. New York: Springer-Verlag, 1983.

Anderson, Eugene. *Self-Esteem for Tots to Teens*. Deephaven, MN: Meadowbrook, 1984.

Anderson, Walter (1975). Pas de psyche. *Human Behavior*, 56–60.

Armstrong, Thomas. *In Their Own Way*. Los Angeles, CA: J. P. Tarcher, 1987.

Batcher, Elaine. *Emotion in the Classroom*. New York: Praeger Press, 1981.

Baum, Susan E. and Cray-Andrews, Martha. *Creativity One, Two, Three: Fostering the Creative Potential of Young Children*. Monroe, NY: Trillium Press, 1988.

Berk, Hilda. *Early Childhood Education: An Introduction*. Buffalo, NY: Prometheus Books, 1988.

Berlay, Louise. *The Magic of the Mind*. Santa Monica, CA: Berle Books, 1986.

Bernstein, Deena and Tiegerman, Ellenmorris. *Language and Communication Disorders in Children*. Columbus, OH: Merrill Publishing, 1989.

Borman, K. M. *The Social Life of Children in a Changing Society*. Hillsdale, NJ: Lawrence Erlbaum Associates, 1982.

Briggs, Dorothy. *Your Child's Self-Esteem: The Key to His Life*. New York: Doubleday, 1975.

Bruner, Jerome. *Child's Talk: Learning to Use the Language*. New York: Norton, 1985.

Bryant, Margaret (1987). Meeting the needs of gifted first-grade children in a heterogenous classroom. *Roeper Review*, 9 (4) 214-216.

Budden, Michael (1989). How not to draw a tree: Stifling creativity is like stifling life itself. *Reading Improvement*, 26 (1) 21–23.

Bunker, Linda. *Motivating Kids Through Play*. Champaign, IL: Leisure Press, 1982.

Campbell, Ross. *How to Really Know Your Child*. Wheaton, IL: Victor Books, 1988.

Carey, Susan. *Conceptual Change in Childhood*. Cambridge, MA: MIT Press, 1987.

Chess, Stella and Thomas, Alexander. *Temperament in Clinical Practice*. Los Angeles, CA: Western Psychological Services, 1989.

Cooley, Vivien. *Time for Snails and Painting Whales: Great Ways to Teach and Enjoy Your Young Children*. Chicago, IL: Moody Press, 1987.

Crabbe, Ann B. *New Directions in Creativity Research*. Los Angeles, CA: National State Leadership Training Institute on the Gifted and Talented, 1986.

Crooker, Lester. *Jean-Jacques Rousseau: The Prophetic Voice*. New York: Macmillan, 1973.

Czeschlik, Tatiana and Rost, Detlef (1989). The relationship of teacher perceptions of child temperament and intellectual ability. Paper presented at the Biennial Meeting of the Society for Research in Child Development, Kansas City, MO.

Espenak, Liljan. *Dance Therapy*. Springfield, IL: Charles C Thomas, 1981.

Fisher, Elaine Flory. *Aesthetic Awareness and the Child*. Itasca, IL: Peacock Publishers, 1978.

Frye, Northrop. *Creation and Recreation*. Toronto: University of Toronto Press, 1980.

Gruber, Howard. *Darwin on Man: A Psychological Study of Scientific Creativity*. Chicago, IL: University of Chicago Press, 1981.

Guilford, J. P. *The Nature of Human Intelligence*. New York: McGraw-Hill, 1967.

Hendrick, Joanne. *Whole Child: Early Education for the Eighties*. Columbus, OH: Merrill Publishing, 1984.

Holt, K. S. *Movement and Child Development*. New York: J. B. Lippincott, 1975.

Humphrey, James H. *Child Development and Learning Through Dance*. New York: AMS Press, 1987.

Johnson, James E., et al. *Play and Early Childhood*. Glenview, IL: Scott Foresman, 1987.

Jones, Barbara S. *Movement Themes: Topics for Early Childhood Learning Through Creative Movement*. Saratoga, CA: R & E Publishers, 1981.

Kagan, Jerome. *Nature of the Child*. New York: Basic Books, 1986.

Keeshan, Bob. *Captain Kangaroo Tells Yesterday's Children How to Nurture Their Own.* New York: Doubleday, 1989.

Laban, Rudolf. *The Mastery of Movement.* London: McDonald & Evans, 1950.

Leach, Penelope. *Your Baby and Child: From Birth Through Age Five.* New York: Alfred A. Knopf, 1980.

Le Shan, Eda. *What Makes Me Feel This Way?* New York: Macmillan, 1972.

Lowrey, George H. *Growth and Development of Children.* Chicago, IL: Year Book Medical Publishers, 1986.

Lynch-Fraser, Diane. *Babysignals.* New York: Walker and Company, 1987.

———. *DancePlay: Creative Movement for Very Young Children.* New York: Walker and Company, 1982.

———. *Getting Ready to Read.* New York: New American Library, 1985.

McKisson, Micki. *Chrysalis: Nurturing Creative and Independent Thought in Children.* Tucson, AZ: Zephyr Press, 1983.

Marland, Sydney (1972). Education of the Gifted and Talented, volume 2. Background papers submitted to the U.S. Department of Education. Washington, DC: U.S. Government Printing Office.

Montessori, Maria. *The Absorbent Mind.* New York: Dell Publishing, 1967.

———. *The Discovery of the Child.* New York: Ballantine Books, 1967.

Newman, Robert E. *God Bless the Grass: Studies in Helping Children Grow in Self-Esteem.* Saratoga, CA: R & E Publishers, 1981.

Pacheco, Anne (1989). Turning on their headlights. *Momentum,* 20 (2) 54–56.

Piaget, Jean. *The Construction of Reality in the Child.* New York: Basic Books, 1954.

———. *The Origins of Intelligence in Children.* New York: Norton, 1963.

Ristow, Robert (1988). The teaching of thinking skills: does it improve creativity? *Gifted Child Today,* 11 (2) 44–46.

Rosenberg, Ellen. *Getting Closer: Discover and Understand Your Child's Secret Feelings About Growing Up.* New York: Berkley Publishing Group, 1985.

Rubin, Judith. *Child Art Therapy: Understanding and Helping Children Through Art.* New York: Van Nostrand Reinhold, 1984.

Sanoff, Henry and Sanoff, Joan. *Learning Environments for Young Children.* Atlanta, GA: Humanics Limited, 1988.

Satir, Virginia. *Conjoint Family Therapy.* Palo Alto, CA: Science and Behavior Books, 1967.

Sawyers, Janet K. and Rogers, Cosby. *Helping Young Children Develop Through Play*. New York: National Association for the Education of Young Children, 1988.

Segal, Marilyn and Adcock, D. *Feelings*. Atlanta, GA: Humanics Limited, 1981.

Smith, Ross. *Eureka: The Six Stages of Creativity*. New York: Simon & Schuster, 1986.

Strom, Robert D. *Growing Through Play: Reading for Parents and Teachers*. Monterey, CA: Brooks-Cole, 1980.

Suzuki, Shinichi. *Nurtured by Love: The Classic Approach to Talent Education*. Smithtown, NY: Exposition Press, 1983.

Thorton, Leonard M. *Growing Up to Become a Child*. Farmingdale, NY: Coleman Publishing, 1986.

Torrance, Paul E. (1972). Can we teach children to think creatively? *Journal of Creative Behavior*, 114–143.

Webb, Patricia K. *The Emerging Child*. New York: Macmillan, 1988.

Winter, Gwen (1988). Interdisciplinary strategies for teaching second-grade gifted children in the regular classroom: an inservice for teachers. Practicum Report, Nova University, Fort Lauderdale, FL.

◇ *INDEX* ◇

Age, 8, 9, 22, 24, 98. *See also* Development;
    Level I exercises; Level II exercises
Animals, 107–8
Attention span, 25, 27, 88

Baby Dance, 52–53
Balance, Balance, 39–40
Balloon-Man, 70–71
Belonging, 95–96, 98
Be Someone Else, 105–6
Body
    control of the, 34
    and the curriculum, 39–42
    and development stages, 12
    exercises for, 36–43
    and the gifted, 113
    and individuality, 34–35, 42–43
    and interpersonal skills, 97–98
    and language development, 65–66, 88
    and relaxation, 36–37, 40–42
    and self-awareness/-image, 9, 34, 43, 49, 64
    and touch, 37, 38
Body Finding, 37–38
Body Prints, 54–55
Body Sculpture, 103–5
Book Report, 83–84, 85
Breathing In and Out, 36–37

Can You Come With Me?, 49–50
Cartoons, 105–6
Choices, 27, 98, 109, 113
Classroom, 12–19, 27–30, 96, 113
Collaboration/cooperation, 96, 102, 103–5
Conformity, 24, 111
Content areas, 28, 30– 31, 113. *See also name of
    specific content area*
Contrasts, 46, 108–9

Control, 9, 27, 29, 34, 95
Costume, 56–57
Creative process
    and adult roles/attitudes, 21–22, 25–26, 29,
        30, 32, 33
    as child-centered, 21, 27, 29
    and the classroom, 27–30
    and content area/curriculum, 25–27, 28,
        30–31
    and control, 27, 29
    definition of the, 23
    and experiences, 24, 25–26, 31
    and fantasy, 23, 24
    and individuality, 30
    and information, 24, 26–27
    and interpersonal skills, 30
    and language development, 30
    as learned, 24
    phases of the, 30–33
    and questions/answers, 24, 30–31, 32
    and reinforcement, 24, 25–26
    and resources, 28, 29–30
    and self-awareness, 30
    starting the, 27–30
Creativity
    and adults' role/attitudes, 110–11, 114
    as an aim of playdancing, 7
    benefits of, 9–10
    and conformity, 111
    and the decline in creative activity, 17
    importance of, 114
    and individuality, 110
    and political activism, 114
    undervaluation of, 111
    See also Creative process; Critical thinking
Critical thinking, 8–9, 23–24, 25–27, 67–68, 114
Crying, 22

Curiosity, 21, 113
Curriculum, 10, 17. *See also* Content areas;
    name of specific content area/curriculum

Dancing Words, 81–82
Development
    manipulative stage of, 11–14
    representational stage of, 17–20
    symbolic stage of, 14–16
    See also name of specific type of development
Disruptive behavior, 28,
    29, 94
Diversity, 47, 106–7, 111
Dramatic play, 47–48, 56–57, 100–102,
    107–8

Eight-year-olds, 17–20.
    See also Level II exercises
Emotions, 19, 62–64, 98,
    100, 102–3
Empathy, 105–7, 108–9
Evaluation, 30, 32–33
Exercises. *See* Level I exercises; Level II
    exercises
Experiences
    and body movement, 35–36
    and the creative process, 24, 25–26, 31
    externalizing of, 35–36
    and the gifted, 111–12
    and interpersonal skills, 98, 109
    and language development, 66, 88
    and self–awareness, 45–46, 48

Failure, 26–27
Fantasy, 8, 9, 23, 24, 47
Finger Friends, 100–102
Five year olds, 14–16. *See also*
    Level I exercises
Four year olds, 11–14. *See also*
    Level I exercises Friendships
    and choosing friends, 98
    and creativity, 111
    exercise about, 100–102
    importance of, 92–98
    learning to make, 91–92

Gifted children, 110–13

Haiku, 82–83
How Could You . . . ?, 59–60
Human Emotion, 62–64

Idea awareness, 30–31
Idea formation, 30, 32

Idea reflection, 30, 32–33
Imaging, 35, 36–37, 67–68
Individuality
    and bodies, 34–35, 42–43
    and creativity, 30, 110
    and giftedness, 110–13
    and interpersonal skills, 89–90, 93, 94–95, 98,
        109
    and self-awareness, 45, 47, 48–49
Information, 24, 26–27, 68, 88, 112
Insecurity, 23–24
Interpersonal skills
    adults' role in developing, 90, 91, 92, 93–94,
        97–98
    and age, 98
    and belonging, 95–96, 98
    and the body, 97–98
    and choices, 98, 109
    and the classroom, 96
    and collaboration, 102, 103–5
    and the creative process, 30
    and critical thinking, 8–9
    development of, 98, 102
    and diversity, 106–7
    and emotions, 98, 100, 102–3
    and empathy, 105–7, 108–9
    exercises for, 99–109
    and experiences, 98, 109
    and the gifted, 111–12
    and individuality, 89–90, 93, 94–95,
        98, 109
    and labeling, 94
    and language development, 88, 100–102,
        105–6, 108–9
    and learning, 92
    and listening, 91, 98, 100
    methods of acquiring, 92
    and modeling, 92, 98
    nurturing of, 97–98
    and passive/active interaction, 103–5
    and peer communication, 95–96
    and perspective taking, 102, 105–8
    and play, 96, 98, 102, 107–8
    and popularity, 90
    and problem solving, 92
    and reciprocity, 98, 102
    and self-awareness, 8, 92, 93–94, 95, 96, 97,
        109
    and sharing, 98, 99–100, 108–9
    and socialization, 96–97
    and social types, 92–94
    and sounds, 100
    and temperament scales, 94
    underutilized/misdirected, 95
    See also Friendships

Labeling, 94
Language development
adults' role in, 66, 88
and the body, 65–66, 88
and the creative process, 30
and critical thinking, 8–9, 67–68
differences between adults and children in, 66–67
exercises for, 70–88
and experiences, 66, 88
and the gifted, 112
and imaging, 67–68
importance of, 66, 67
and information, 68–69, 88
and interpersonal skills, 88, 100–102, 105–6, 108–9
and learning, 66, 67
and play, 68–69
and problem solving, 67, 88
process, 69–70, 79–80
and rhymes/rhythm, 72–73, 75
and self-awareness, 49–51, 52–53, 57–58, 61, 66, 88
Learning
from adults, 88, 96–97
beginning of, 22
and the creative process, 24
and development stages, 12, 17–20
and emotions, 19
and interpersonal skills, 91–92
and language development, 66, 67
and movement, 17
from peers, 88, 96–97
and self-awareness, 48
Letter Learning, 75–77
Level I exercises
and body discovery, 36–39
characteristics of, 9
and the curriculum, 10
and interpersonal skills, 99–102
and language development, 70–80
and self-awareness, 9, 49–58
Level II exercises
and body discovery, 39–43
characteristics of, 9
and the curriculum, 10
and interpersonal skills, 102–9
and language development, 80–88
and self-awareness, 9, 59–64
Listening, 26, 91, 98, 100

Manipulative stage, 11–14
Masks, 106–7
Mathematics, 53–54
Memory, 88, 112

Me and My Shadow, 38
Modeling, 92, 98
Movie Review, 86–87
Moving in Space, 53–54
Music, 8, 62–64, 113. *See also name of specific exercise*
Musical Pictures, 71–72
My Favorite Things, 57–58

Nursery Rhymes, 72–73

Opposites, 108–9

Parents
and creativity, 21–22, 25, 30, 32, 110–11, 114
and development, 20
and the gifted, 112
and interpersonal skills, 90, 91, 92, 93–94, 97
and language development, 66–67, 88
learning from, 96–97
and self-awareness, 88
Peers, 88, 96–97. *See also* Interpersonal skills
Perspective taking, 102, 105–8
Picture Box, 77–78
Play
dramatic, 47–48, 56–57, 100–102, 107–8
and interpersonal skills, 96, 98, 100–102, 107–8
and language development, 68–69
symbolic, 68–69
Playdancing
tenets/components of, 7–10
Political activism, 114
Problem solving, 7, 25–27, 64, 67, 88, 92, 113

Quiet Place, 51–52

Reciprocity, 98, 102
Reinforcement, 24, 25–26
Relaxation, 36–37, 40–42
Representational stage, 17–20
Rhymes/rhythm, 37, 49, 72–73, 75
Rhyming Rhythms, 75

Science curriculum, 17, 39–40, 51–52, 58, 107–8
Sculpture, 103–5
Self-actualization, 109
Self-awareness
adults' role in developing, 45, 46
and age, 8, 9
and the body, 9, 49, 64
and contrasts, 46
and control, 9
and the creative process, 30
and critical thinking, 8–9
and the curriculum, 51–52, 56–57, 58, 62–64

Self-awareness *(Continued)*
  definition of, 8, 45
  and development, 20
  development of, 48–49
  and dramatic play, 47–48, 56–57
  and emotions, 62–64
  exercises for, 9, 49–64
  and experiences, 45–46, 48
  and fantasy, 8, 47
  and individuality, 45, 47, 48
  and interpersonal skills, 8, 109
  and language development, 49–51, 52–53,
    57–58, 61, 66, 88
  and learning, 48
  phases of, 48–49
  and problem solving, 64
  and rhyme/rhythm, 49
  role of dance in, 44
  and separation/individuation, 48–49
  and sound/silence, 45–46, 51–52
  and space, 45–46, 53–54, 60
  and time, 45–46
Self-confidence, 95
Self-constancy, 48–51, 54–55
Self-control, 95
Self-differentiation, 48–51, 53–55, 58, 60
Self-esteem, 48–50, 52–53, 57–58, 62–64, 94, 95,
  109
Self-identity
  in ages six to eight, 59–64
  in ages three to five, 48–49, 50–58
Self-image, 19, 22, 34, 43, 92, 93–94, 97
Self-indication, 96
Separation/individuation, 48–49
Seven year olds, 17–20. *See also* Level II
  exercises
Sharing, 98, 99–100, 102–3, 108–9
Silence, 46, 51–52
Six year olds, 14–16. *See also* Level II exercises
Social interaction. *See* Interpersonal skills
Socialization, 96–97. *See also* Interpersonal
  skills

Social studies curriculum, 17, 40–42, 56–57,
  62–64
Social types, 92–94
Something Special, 84–86
Sound, 45–46, 51–52, 100
Space, 45–46, 53–54, 60
Space Patterns, 60
Story Box, 78–79
Storytelling, 79, 113
Symbolic play, 68–69
Symbolic stage, 14–16

Take a Good Look, 42–43
Talented children, 110–13
Talking Tapes, 73–74
Teachers, self-image of, 22
Teachers' role
  and creativity, 21–22, 25–26, 29, 30, 32, 33,
    110–11, 114
  and development, 20
  and the gifted, 112
  and interpersonal skills, 91, 93–94, 97–98
  and language development, 66–67, 88
  and self-awareness, 45, 46
Temperament scales, 94
Textures, 58
Three year olds, 11–14, 93. *See also* Level I
  exercises
Tied Together, 99–100
Time, 45–46
Touch, 37, 38, 100
Touching Others, 100
Tracings, 50–51

Vacation Spots, 87

Walk Like the Animal, 107–8
Weather Report, 61
What Do You See?, 102–3
Writing, 8, 83–84, 85

Yoga, 40–42